EDITORIAL DIRECTOR   Carol Francis, Julie A. Schumacher
EXECUTIVE EDITOR   Jim Strickler
SENIOR EDITOR   Terry Ofner
EDITORIAL TEAM   Ken Sidey, Lucy Anello, Sheri Cooper, Terry Ofner,
                          Rebecca Christian, Andrea Stark
ART DIRECTOR   Randy Messer
DESIGN TEAM   Tobi Cunningham, Deborah Bell
RESEARCH ASSISTANT   Ashley Kuehl
WRITER   Pegi Bevins
PERMISSIONS   Laura Pieper

COVER ART SEATED GIRL WITH DOG 1944 Milton Avery, Roy R. Neuberger Collection.
© 1999 Milton Avery Trust/Artists Rights Society (ARS), New York.

 4 5 6 7 QG 18 17 16 15 14 13

78690
ISBN: 978-0-7891-5122-3

Printed in the United States of America

TABLE OF CONTENTS

ADDITIONAL RESOURCES

The Common Core State Standards and *Literature & Thought*

Throughout this Teacher Guide, you will see many references to specific Common Core State Standards. The program as a whole, however, has been helping students achieve the broader, overarching goals of the standards, as expressed in the Introduction and the Anchor Standards in the *CCSS for English Language Arts,* since long before the standards were even published.

Text Complexity Selections in *Literature & Thought* anthologies cover a range of lengths and reading levels. This range encourages students to "read and comprehend complex literary and informational texts" and grow into independent readers. (Reading Anchor Standard 10)

Close Reading With readings from a variety of genres and points of view, the program fosters the "close, attentive reading that is at the heart of understanding and enjoying complex works of literature." (Reading Anchor Standard 1)

Reading for a Purpose The question that ties together the readings in each cluster and the essential question of the entire book encourage students to "perform the critical reading" needed to sort through information for a purpose. (Reading Anchor Standard 9)

Text-Dependent Questions The questions in both the Student Book and the Teacher Guide call for turning to the text itself for answers. (Reading Anchor Standard 1)

Claims, Reasoning, and Evidence The program's emphasis on finding evidence to support interpretations and answers helps build "cogent reasoning," an essential skill for both personal and public life. (Reading Anchor Standard 8)

Collaborative Discussions The discussion questions provided in the Teacher Guide for each selection create opportunities for "rich, structured conversations." (Speaking and Listening Anchor Standard 1)

Direct Engagement With a minimum of instructional apparatus, *Literature & Thought* anthologies allow students to engage directly with high-quality texts that broaden their knowledge and worldview. (Reading Anchor Standard 9)

Meanings of Words and Phrases The Vocabulary lists in the Teacher Guide that appear at the beginning of each cluster and each selection, combined with Vocabulary Tests at the end of each cluster, help students "determine technical, connotative, and figurative meanings" of words and phrases. (Reading Anchor Standard 4)

Points of View Selections within a cluster provide a range of points of view about one central question. This variety enables students to "analyze how two or more texts address similar themes or topics" and to assess the significance of point of view. (Reading Anchor Standards 6 and 9)

Research Projects and Technology The Research, Writing, and Discussion Topics and the Assessment and Project Ideas in the Teacher Guide provide ample opportunities for students to "use technology, including the Internet," to "conduct short as well as more sustained research projects," and to "write routinely over extended time frames." (Writing Anchor Standards 6, 7, 10)

Projects The Rubric for Project Evaluation in the Teacher Guide is designed to help students create projects that meet or exceed the Common Core State Standards for their grade level. (Speaking and Listening Standards 4–6)

The Common Core State Standards Correlations

Correlations aligning *Who Am I?* to the Common Core State Standards for English Language Arts are included in the digital version of the Teacher Guide on the enclosed CD. Selected items in the Teacher Guide with especially strong standard support are labeled by strand, grade level range, and standard number, and the label is highlighted in gray. For example, the label *(RI.8–12.4)* indicates that an item addresses the Reading Informational Text strand (RI), grades 8–12, standard 4. The correlations and labels use these abbreviations:

Names of the Standards		Additional Abbreviations	
RL	ELA Reading Literature	**ELA**	English Language Arts
RI	ELA Reading Informational Text	**SB**	Student Book
W	ELA Writing	**TG**	Teacher Guide
SL	ELA Speaking and Listening	**IWL**	Interactive Whiteboard Lesson

When using the digital version, click on the link below to open a correlation. To identify questions and activities that address a standard, choose the correlation for that grade level and strand. To identify all the standards that a selection addresses, choose the Standards Correlated by Selection for a grade level.

Grade 6 Correlations
6 ELA Reading Literature
6 ELA Reading Informational Text
6 ELA Writing
6 ELA Speaking and Listening
6 Standards Correlated by Selection

Grade 7 Correlations
7 ELA Reading Literature
7 ELA Reading Informational Text
7 ELA Writing
7 ELA Speaking and Listening
7 Standards Correlated by Selection

Grade 8 Correlations
8 ELA Reading Literature
8 ELA Reading Informational Text
8 ELA Writing
8 ELA Speaking and Listening
8 Standards Correlated by Selection

Grades 9–10 Correlations
9–10 ELA Reading Literature
9–10 ELA Reading Informational Text
9–10 ELA Writing
9–10 ELA Speaking and Listening
9–10 Standards Correlated by Selection

Grades 11–12 Correlations
11–12 ELA Reading Literature
11–12 ELA Reading Informational Text
11–12 ELA Writing
11–12 ELA Speaking and Listening
11–12 Standards Correlated by Selection

Features of the Student Book

Introducing the Theme

Preface The Preface introduces the student to the essential question of the book. This question, together with the cluster questions and thinking skills, will guide student reading throughout the anthology. Use the Preface to set a purpose for reading.

Prologue The Prologue combines a strong visual image with a thematically relevant quotation. The Prologue is designed to stimulate discussion and to set the tone for study of the anthology.

Creating Context The Creating Context section uses a combination of text and graphics to create a framework for learning and to provide for assessing prior knowledge. The final page of this section is a Concept Vocabulary list that provides definitions for important content-related terms that students may not be familiar with.

The Selections

Clusters The anthology is divided into four clusters of selections. The selections offer a mixture of historical and contemporary writings. They provide opportunities for students to meet the Common Core State Standards by reading and comprehending complex literary and informational texts. The more complex selections tend to be short in order to facilitate close study and rereading.

Cluster Questions and Critical Thinking Skills The selections in all but the last cluster are grouped around a cluster question and critical thinking skill, which are stated on the cluster opening page. Reading the selections in the cluster will help students answer the cluster question as well as exercise the critical thinking skill.

Responding to the Cluster Rather than interrupting the flow of reading with questions after every selection, *Literature & Thought* anthologies present discussion questions at the end of the cluster. Questions often address multiple selections, encouraging students to compare and synthesize. Most questions address the Common Core State Standards.

Writing Activity Each of the first three clusters ends with a writing activity that integrates the cluster question with the cluster thinking skill. The writing activity is correlated to the Common Core State Standards.

The Final Cluster

The Final Cluster Having practiced several thinking skills and with a core of selections behind them, students should be able to approach the final cluster of selections independently.

Features of This Teacher Guide

Common Core State Standards Labels All questions, activities, and other elements of the Teacher Guide that address the Common Core State Standards are identified in the correlation charts available on the enclosed CD. Selected items in the Teacher Guide with especially strong standard support are labeled by strand, grade level range, and standard number, and the label is highlighted in gray. For example, the label *(RI.8–12.4)* indicates that the item addresses the Reading Informational Text strand (RI), grades 8–12, standard 4. Abbreviations are defined on page 6.

Planning and Scheduling Options Use these strategies for planning a 4- to 6-week unit, a 1- to 2-week unit, or using the student book in conjunction with another resource.

What Do You Know? (Anticipation Guide) To assess your students' attitudes toward the essential question of this anthology, administer the anticipation guide on page 66.

Introducing the Theme These strategies include resources for teaching the Preface to set the purpose for reading; the Prologue for setting the tone of the theme study; and the Creating Context section for setting the framework, or context, of the book.

Teaching the Critical Thinking Skill Each cluster in the Teacher Guide begins with a lesson plan and handout for modeling the cluster thinking skill. The handout is also available as a whiteboard lesson. A second whiteboard lesson provides more detailed support for developing the critical thinking skill.

Cluster Vocabulary Handouts and Tests Students can use the reproducible vocabulary sheets to reference challenging words in each selection and to prepare for the Cluster Vocabulary Tests.

Selection Resources Every selection in the student book is enhanced with the following teacher supports: selection summaries, reading hints, thinking skills, extension activities, discussion questions with suggested answers, and additional notes and activities.

Responding to the Cluster This resource page provides sample answers to the cluster questions that appear in the student book.

Writing Activity Reproducible Sheet This graphic organizer integrates the writing activity and the cluster critical thinking skill. It is also available as an interactive whiteboard lesson. A second whiteboard lesson provides a rubric tied to the type of writing developed in the activity.

Suggestions for Teaching the Final Cluster The final cluster provides an opportunity for students to demonstrate their mastery of the content knowledge and thinking skills.

The Essay Prompt This open-book essay prompt is based on the book's essential question. Use it as a culminating essay test. Preceding the prompt is a page to prepare students to write the essay.

Rubric for Project Evaluation Use or adapt these rubrics for assessing student projects. Separate rubrics are available for grades 6–8, 9–10, and 11–12.

Features of the Interactive Whiteboard Lessons

Four types of interactive whiteboard lessons accompany each cluster. Depending on each classroom's needs and resources, the lessons can be displayed on a whiteboard for whole-class activities or used for small-group work on computers.

Introducing the Cluster Thinking Skill This whiteboard lesson offers the option to display for the whole class the activity on the reproducible page at the beginning of each cluster in the Teacher Guide. It provides an opportunity to introduce the cluster critical thinking skill before students have begun to read selections in the cluster.

Developing the Cluster Thinking Skill Closely aligned to the Common Core State Standards, this lesson "unpacks" the sub-skills involved in the cluster thinking skill and provides rich examples for students to practice all aspects of the skills. This lesson is designed for use when students are beginning the cluster, or at any time during their study of it.

Cluster-Closing Writing Activity This lesson offers the option to display for the whole class the writing activity and graphic organizer that concludes each cluster. It provides an excellent way to introduce the writing activity whenever students begin to work on it, either before or after they have read the selections in the cluster.

Writing Rubric Building on the outcomes described in the Common Core State Standards for argumentative, explanatory, and narrative writing, these rubrics can serve as both a guide to students as they write and an assessment tool for peers and the teacher. They can be used with the cluster writing activity or with any other writing assignment.

In addition, the last cluster of the book includes a fifth whiteboard lesson.

Teaching the Cluster The final cluster suggests alternative approaches to the study of the selections. It presents various teaching options designed to promote independent work by students.

Assessments

Discussing the Selection Discussion questions assess student comprehension of each selection and build speaking and listening skills.

Responding to the Cluster The questions on the Responding to the Cluster pages can be used to assess student mastery of the cluster content and the cluster thinking skill.

Cluster Vocabulary Tests These 10-point vocabulary tests assess student understanding of key vocabulary words.

Writing Activities Writing activities are ideal for assessing student understanding of the content and thinking skill of each cluster.

Essay Prompt Use the final essay prompt to assess student understanding of the essential question of the theme study.

Rubric for Project Evaluation This rubric, based on the Common Core State Standards, can be used to assess a wide variety of student projects.

Writing Rubric One whiteboard lesson for each cluster is a writing rubric based on the Common Core State Standards for argumentative, explanatory, or narrative writing.

Three Teaching Options for *Who Am I?*

4- TO 6-WEEK UNIT

Page Numbers in

Student Book   Teacher Guide

Introducing the theme (1 to 2 days)

Read and discuss the following sections
- What Do You Know? (anticipation guide) 13, 66
- Preface 3 12
- Prologue 4–5 12
- Creating Context 9–10 14

Teaching the first three clusters (3 to 5 days per cluster)
- Introduce and model the cluster thinking
  skill using whiteboard lesson/handout 15, 27, 38
- Pass out cluster vocabulary sheet 17, 29, 40
- Set schedule for reading selections in first three clusters
- For each selection, use appropriate discussion
  questions and extension activities
  Cluster One 12–45 18–23
  Cluster Two 48–73 30–34
  Cluster Three 76–109 41–44
- As a class or in small groups discuss the **Responding
  to the Cluster** questions . . . . 46, 74, 110 . . . . 24, 35, 45
- Introduce Writing Activity with handout 25, 36, 46
- Administer Vocabulary Test 26, 37, 47

Teaching the last cluster (5 to 10 days)

The final section can be structured as a teacher-directed cluster or as independent learning.
Choose from the two models described below.

Teacher-Directed
- Introduce and model the cluster thinking
  skill using whiteboard lesson 49
- Pass out cluster vocabulary sheet 51
- Set schedule for reading selections
- For each selection, use appropriate discussion
  questions and extension activities 52–56
- Introduce Writing Activity with whiteboard lesson . . . . IWL 4.3
- Administer Vocabulary Test 57
- Assign research projects 58, 59
- Prepare for final essay test 60
- Administer final essay test 61

Independent Learning

Have students
- respond to one or more of the questions or activities
  on the **Responding to Cluster Four** page 143
- plan and present a lesson over one or more of the
  selections in the last cluster 112–142
- conduct additional research on a related topic 58, 59

Three Teaching Options for *Who Am I?*

1- TO 2-WEEK UNIT

Shorten the 4- to 6-week schedule by using one or more of the following strategies.

- Assign complete clusters to literary circles. Have each group share what they learn and/or teach the cluster to their classmates.
- Assign individual selections to groups. Have each group share what they learn and/or teach the selection to the entire class.
- Choose 8–10 significant selections for study by the entire class. The following list would provide a shortened exploration of the themes in the *Who Am I?* anthology.

Title	Page	Title	Page
Remember Me	12	Born Worker	76
Your Body Is Your ID	28	Dolly's False Legacy	86
Be-ers and Doers	34	I'm Nobody	109
Tiffany, age eleven	48	Side 32	125
The Green Killer	52	Birthday Box	138

USING *WHO AM I?* WITH RELATED LITERATURE

Before Reading the Related Work

- Introduce the theme and the purpose for reading using the Anticipation Guide (page 66 of this teacher guide). From the *Who Am I?* anthology use the Preface (page 3), the Prologue (pages 4–5), and Creating Context (pages 9–10).
- Have students choose one or two selections and a poem to read from each cluster. Ask students to report on their selection and how it helped them answer the cluster question.

During Reading

- Ask students to relate the readings in the *Who Am I?* anthology to themes, actions, or statements in the longer work.
- At strategic points, have students discuss how characters in the longer work would react to selections in the anthology.

After Reading

- Have students read the last cluster and respond to the cluster questions, drawing upon selections in the anthology as well as the longer work.
- Ask students to compare and contrast one or more selections in the anthology and a theme in the longer work.
- Allow students to choose a research topic from the options given in **Research, Writing, and Discussion Topics** (page 58) or **Assessment and Project Ideas** (page 59).

Related Works

The following works are Common Core Exemplar Texts that are available from Perfection Learning.

The Joy Luck Club by Amy Tan. Chronicles the 40-year friendship of four Chinese women through vignettes from the lives of the women and their daughters. [RL 8.4 IL 9–12] Paperback 2814601; Cover Craft 2814601.

Their Eyes Were Watching God by Zora Neale Hurston. A classic of black literature, it tells the story of Janie Crawford's evolving sense of self. [RL 7.9 IL 9–12] Paperback 2798901; Cover Craft 2798902.

Woman Hollering Creek by Sandra Cisneros. A collection of stories set on both sides of the Mexican border, by the award-winning author of *The House on Mango Street*. [RL 7.0 IL 9–12] Paperback 4635001; Cover Craft 4635002.

See page 65 of this guide for a more complete list of related titles.

Teaching the Preface (page 3)

WHO'S THE REAL YOU?

The question above is the *essential question* that your students will consider as they read the *Who Am I?* anthology. The literature, activities, and organization of the book will lead them to think critically about this question and to develop a deeper understanding of who they are.

To help students shape their answers to the broad essential question, they will read and respond to four sections, or clusters. Each cluster addresses a specific question and thinking skill.

CLUSTER ONE How do I find out who I am? **DEFINE**

CLUSTER TWO Where do I fit? **ANALYZE**

CLUSTER THREE What do I believe? **EVALUATE**

CLUSTER FOUR Thinking on your own **SYNTHESIZE**

Notice that the final cluster asks students to think independently about their answers to the essential question—*Who's the real you?*

Discussing the Preface Review the Preface with students. Point out the essential question as well as the cluster questions addressed in each cluster. You may want to revisit the essential question after students complete each cluster. The last cluster addresses the essential question directly.

Teaching the Prologue (pages 4–5)

Discussing the Image
- What does the image convey to you about the theme of identity?
- Why is it blurry?

Discussing the Poem
- What does the speaker need to feel cool and in control?
- Where is the poet using figurative language?
- What does the poet mean by "find my right mask"?
- Why does the speaker need to go through this process to attend a party?

What Do You Know? (Anticipation Guide)

Use the reproducible anticipation guide on page 66 of this teacher guide to assess your students' attitudes toward the theme of identity.

_____ 1. Your personality stays basically the same throughout your life.

_____ 2. The way people treat you affects who you think you are.

_____ 3. It's really important to fit in with other people.

_____ 4. You should say what you really think, no matter what.

_____ 5. It feels good to be popular.

_____ 6. If you are yourself, people will like you.

_____ 7. It's easier to get friends when you are going steady.

_____ 8. Being adopted makes it more difficult to find out who you are.

_____ 9. It's natural for people to be mean to unattractive people.

_____10. Smart people aren't popular.

Teaching the Creating Context Section (pages 9–10)

Use these Creating Context features to activate students' prior knowledge and build background about their attitudes toward the theme of identity.

Living the Examined Life: An Inside Job (page 9) This essay offers a hypothetical situation that allows students to imagine having an opportunity to re-create their identities. It then explores the foundation to identity, and the importance of flexibility and introspection.

Discussing the Essay

- What is an identity? Work on a tentative whole-class definition. Refer to it as you work your way through the anthology; edit it as the class's definition evolves.
- What are some ways that we can examine our lives?
- What are some ways we are rewarded for living the "examined life"?

Concept Vocabulary (page 10) The terms on this page are important to understanding the idea of identity.

Discussing Concept Vocabulary

- Discuss terms that may be new to students.
- Have students record new concept words in a journal as they read the anthology.

CLUSTER ONE

Defining

I. Present this definition to students.

   Defining is explaining the meaning of a word or concept.

II. Discuss with students how they already use defining by sharing the situations below.

   You define when you
   - answer a child's question about what a word means
   - explain what you mean by *out of bounds* when you play a game
   - learn a technical term like *photosynthesis* by stating its meaning in your own words
   - discuss whether your idea of identity is the same as someone else's

   You might invite students to suggest other situations where defining could be used.

III. Explain to students that the selections they will be reading contain diverse characters who experience their identities in different ways. Use the following steps to show how to begin developing a definition of identity in order to investigate the question "Who Am I?"

   A. Use the reproducible "Defining Identity" on the next page as a blackline master or use the interactive whiteboard lesson, WhoAmI_1.1_CriticalThink.

   B. Discuss how Vivian Vande Velde explores identity when she writes in the voice of a man who has lost his.

   C. Ask students to begin developing their own definitions of identity. Have them complete **Organizer B** by jotting down what they think *identity* means and listing examples of what identity is and what it is not. Tell students that this is only a beginning—their ideas may change as they read. *(RL.6–12.4, RI.6–12.4)*

For additional in-depth work on developing the skill of defining, see the interactive whiteboard lesson, WhoAmI_1.2_CCSSThinking. *(RL.6–12.4, RI.6–12.4)*

Defining Identity

Cluster Question: How do I find out who I am?

Directions: The excerpt in **Organizer A** below is from "Remember Me" by Vivian Vande Velde. It conveys a young prince's feelings when he realizes he has lost his memory and, therefore, his identity. Look for the ways the prince searches to define, and thus rediscover, who he is. Using **Organizer A** as your model, develop your own definition of identity by jotting down examples of what *you* think identity is and is not in **Organizer B**. Then combine the most important elements in a short, well-structured sentence or two. After reading the selections in the book, you may wish to expand or alter your definition.

Organizer A

Excerpt
My clothes are satin and brocade. I have two rings, one on each hand—one is set with two emeralds; the other is simple gold, in the form of a dragon eating its own tail. I also have a gold clasp for my cloak. *So,* I reason, *I'm a wealthy man.* And, it takes no memory but only common sense to know, wealth means power. But I don't feel powerful, without even having a name. *from* "Remember Me," by Vivian Vande Velde

Examples of What Identity Is: knowing who you are; knowing why you possess certain things; feeling powerful and in control of yourself	**Examples of What Identity Is Not:** having money or expensive things when you don't know what they mean or why you have them; having wealth when you do not know yourself

Organizer B

Examples of What I Think Identity Is:	**Examples of What I Think Identity Is Not:**

My Definition of Identity:

Cluster One Vocabulary

Watch for the following words as you read the selections in Cluster One. Record your own vocabulary words and definitions on the blank lines.

Remember Me pages 12–23

ancestral given by ancestors; handed down from forefathers and foremothers

appraisingly critically; to determine worth or value

arrogant superior-acting; overly proud

console comfort; soothe; encourage

disconsolate hopelessly unhappy; cheerless; gloomy

elude evade; escape by cleverness or speed

legitimate lawful; logical

_____

_____

_____

On Being Seventeen, Bright, and Unable to Read pages 24–27

IQ an abbreviation of Intelligence Quotient, determined through a test

potter's wheel a machine on which potters sculpt pots, bowls, and art out of clay

_____

_____

_____

Your Body Is Your ID pages 28–31

configuration the way things are put together; external form

passé out of date; no longer competitive or useful

pilfered stolen; swiped; taken without permission

_____

_____

_____

The Changeling/Transformación pages 32–33

baffled confused; bewildered

carnage butchery; massacre

vying competing

_____

_____

_____

Be-ers and Doers pages 34–44

afghan a soft, lightweight blanket, usually hand knitted or crocheted

bored drilled; in this context, stared intensely; stared intimidatingly

conformity obedience; submission to norms

contrary contradictory; opposite of what is expected

crocheting a method of weaving with thread or yarn

crooning singing in a low, soothing tone; serenading

embroidering making ornamental designs on cloth with thread and needle

verandah a large porch

_____

_____

_____

Getting Ready page 45

cowlicks tufts of hair that stick out on the head

foraging searching for food; here it means rummaging

_____

_____

_____

Remember Me by Vivian Vande Velde, pages 12–23 Short Story

Summary

A witch casts a spell on a young prince, causing him to lose his memory. He becomes lost, and when he seeks help he is treated with contempt. As he struggles to redefine his identity he gains insight into how commoners live and are treated. Ultimately, he is recognized and restored to his princely status a changed man.

Reading Hint	Thinking Skill	Extension
This selection is a fantasy piece, set in the days of castles, horses, and dragons. Discuss the setting to help orient the students.	Why might the princess have secretly cast this spell on the prince?	**Writing Activity:** Have students choose a character from the story and write a letter to the prince from that character's point of view, explaining how they feel about him now that they know his identity. For example, students could write an apology from the king's steward. *(RL.6–7.6)*

Vocabulary

ancestral given by ancestors; handed down from forefathers and foremothers

appraisingly critically; to determine worth or value

arrogant superior-acting; overly proud

console comfort; soothe; encourage

disconsolate hopelessly unhappy; cheerless; gloomy

elude evade; escape by cleverness or speed

legitimate lawful; logical

Discussing the Short Story

1. How is the prince treated when he first approaches the strange castle? Cite evidence from the text in support of your answer. (Recall) *He is treated with respect and courtesy. People "scurry out of the way of my horse," (p. 14) and "When I get to the gate of the castle itself, guards standing at either side bow . . ." (pp. 14–15). (RL.6–12.1)*

2. How does the prince treat the people of this strange town? (Recall) *He acts honorably. He is polite and honest.*

3. Why do the people at the castle change their attitude toward the prince? (Analysis) *Answers will vary. They have no proof that he really is royalty. They are not required to treat him with respect. (RL.6–12.3)*

4. How is the prince richer for his experience? Cite evidence from the text in support of your answer. (Analysis) *Answers will vary. He now knows how it feels to be treated like a commoner. He understands how it feels to be treated disrespectfully and what it is like to be poor. When he finally returns to his home, his family and friends say that he is "more patient and kinder" (p. 22). (RL.6–12.1, RL.6–12.2)*

Special Focus: Names and Identity

The prince ponders the fact that wealth means power but realizes that he doesn't feel power "without even having a name."

Use the following questions to discuss with students how important they think names are to identity.

- Does your first or last name have any special meaning or give clues to your identity? Explain.

- If you could pick a new name, what name would you choose? Why?

- Are nicknames more descriptive of a person's identity than given names? Why or why not?

Discussing the Image

What do the images on pages 12 and 23 say to you about losing or finding your identity?

On Being Seventeen, Bright, and Unable to Read

by David Raymond, pages 24–27   Autobiography

Summary

A young dyslexic man shares his frustrations and his hopes as he reviews his school years and looks toward his future. He reveals that being unable to read made him feel insecure in many areas, but finding support and encouragement allowed him to move forward in his life.

Reading Hint	Thinking Skill	Extension
Remind students to read the endnote to find out what happened to David after the article was written.	Imagine what your life would be like if suddenly letters were jumbled and you were unable to read.	**Discussion:** Ask the class why they think students sometimes treat each other cruelly.

Vocabulary

IQ an abbreviation of Intelligence Quotient, determined through a test

potter's wheel a machine on which potters sculpt pots, bowls, and art out of clay

Discussing the Autobiography

1. Why was David afraid to learn to ride a bike or swim? (Recall) *He was afraid he would fail.*

2. What did David wish for on his birthdays? (Recall) *He wished for friends.*

3. What might have happened to David if he had never met people who helped him? (Analysis) *Answers will vary. He would have kept feeling bad about himself. He might have dropped out of school or not gone to college. (RI.6.5)*

4. What special insights has David's dyslexia given him? (Analysis) *Answers will vary. He understands how it feels to be left out, made fun of, or misunderstood. He is careful not to treat others that way. (RI.6–12.1)*

Special Focus: Famous Dyslexics

Share with students the list of famous people who were or are dyslexics. Discuss with them how the world would be different today if these people had not found ways to succeed in spite of their learning disability.

Inventors and Scientists: Albert Einstein, Henry Ford, Thomas Edison, Alexander Graham Bell, Leonardo da Vinci

Financial Wizards: Nelson Rockefeller, Charles Schwab

Artists: Leonardo da Vinci, Walt Disney

Performers: George Burns, Cher, Jay Leno, Whoopi Goldberg, Danny Glover

Authors: Hans Christian Andersen, William Butler Yeats

Discussing the Image

Have students write captions for the photograph on page 25 from David's point of view in second grade, in junior high, and in high school. *(RL.6–7.6)*

Your Body Is Your ID by Hank Schlesinger, pages 28–31   Article

Summary

The author defines biometrics, the science of identification through physical characteristics. He explains how the means of identifying people will change drastically in the next century.

Reading Hint	Thinking Skill	Extension
Tell students not to be intimidated by technical terms in this article. Have them study the footnotes for explanations.	What recent inventions would have seemed fascinating and futuristic to people 100 years ago?	**Writing Activity:** Have students write diary entries while pretending the year is a half century from now. The entries should mention technology.

Vocabulary

configuration the way things are put together; external form

passé out of date; no longer competitive or useful

pilfered stolen; swiped; taken without permission

Discussing the Article

1. What parts of the body are vital in biometric identification? (Recall) *The eye, face, voice, finger, and hand are all vital in biometric identification.*

2. What method of biometric identification is the most accurate? (Recall) *Iris scans are the most accurate.*

3. What objections might some people have to biometric identification? (Analysis) *Answers will vary. Some might see a scan of the body as an invasion of privacy. Criminals might see it as particularly threatening.*

4. How might biometric identification make your future more secure? (Analysis) *Answers will vary. It would be harder to steal things, including credit card numbers and cars. It would be harder for someone to break into a house.*

Special Focus: Sophisticated Technology

Discuss with students the social implications of increasingly sophisticated means of identifying people. Use the questions below to prompt discussion. *(SL.6–12.1)*

- In what ways can technology threaten our identities?
- In what ways can technology help us find out who we are?

Discussing the Image

Have students identify the ways the information presented in the graphic on pages 30–31 is different from the information presented in the article. *The graphic goes into more detail about the technology behind each biometric identification technique. (RI.6–10.7)*

The Changeling/Transformación
by Judith Ortíz Cofer/translated from the English by Johanna Vega, pages 32–33   Poem

Summary
The speaker remembers how she dressed up in her brother's clothes and transformed herself into the legendary Che Guevara in order to gain her father's attention. The transformation lasts only until her mother orders her back to her place in the "real world of her kitchen."

Reading Hint	Thinking Skill	Extension
Alert students that this poem was written originally in English, then translated into Spanish. The translation appears on the facing page.	Why do you think the girl feels invisible when she returns to the kitchen?	**Journal Entry:** Have students write in their journals about a time when they felt "invisible."

Vocabulary
baffled confused; bewildered

carnage butchery; massacre

vying competing

Discussing the Poem
1. Why does the young girl invent her dress-up game? (Analysis) *Answers will vary. She wants to get her father's attention. She is expressing her own yearning for power and strength.*

2. How do her parents react to her game? (Recall) *Her father is baffled and amused. He smiles. Her mother does not appreciate it.*

3. Which line or lines from the poem have the most impact? (Analysis) *Answers will vary. Some may point to the lines that evoke the danger and romance of the revolutionary's life; others may point to the final line that brings home the "reality" of the girl's expected role in the family and society. (RL.6–12.1)*

4. What is the main theme of this poem? Cite specific lines to support your answer. (Analysis) *Answers will vary. Clothes do not make the person: "She'd ordered me back to the dark cubicle / that smelled of adventure, to shed my costume, . . ."*

   Fantasy vs. Reality: "She was not amused / by my transformation . . . return invisible, / as myself, / to the real world of her kitchen." (RL.6–12.2)

Special Focus: Trying on Identities
By dressing up in boys' clothes, the speaker in the poem is trying on a hero's identity. Discuss with students the various identities people "try on" while searching for themselves. Use the following questions to prompt discussion. (SL.6–12.1)

- Which is the more effective way of finding out who you are: trying out different roles or identities, or searching inside yourself?
- The girl in the poem "The Changeling" tries on a set of clothes in order to feel the role of a revolutionary. How important are looks to identity?

Special Focus: Figurative Language
The poet uses specific words to evoke gender identities. Have students list and contrast the words used to evoke masculine and feminine gender roles. Discuss with the class the effect of the contrast. (RL.6–12.4)

Be-ers and Doers by Budge Wilson, pages 34–44 Short Story

Summary

Albert grows up with two parents who have very different views about how to live. His mother believes in *doing,* being constantly productive. His father, on the other hand, believes in the importance of simply *being,* of taking time to enjoy life and to philosophize. Albert eventually rebels against his mother's plan for his future and takes on the life of a be-er.

Reading Hint	Thinking Skill	Extension
The setting of the story may be unfamiliar. Have the students find Nova Scotia on a map and locate the places mentioned in the story.	Why do you think Albert waits so long to tell his mother how he feels?	**Discussion:** Ask students if they think Albert finds his true identity at the end of the story or if he is merely rebelling against his mother. *(SL.6–12.1)*

Vocabulary

afghan a soft, lightweight blanket, usually hand knitted or crocheted

bored stared intensely; stared intimidatingly

conformity obedience; submission to norms

contrary contradictory; opposite of what is expected

crocheting a method of weaving with thread or yarn

crooning singing in a low, soothing tone; serenading

embroidering making ornamental designs on cloth with thread and needle

verandah a large porch

Discussing the Short Story

1. What does the mother expect of Albert when he is born? (Recall) *She expects that he will be a* doer.

2. The mother told her children, "Me, I'm a doer." Cite a passage in which the author shows the mother "doing." (Analysis) *Answers will vary. "She'd huff, and disappear into the house, clattering pans, thumping the mop. . ." (p. 37). (RL.6–12.1)*

3. How is the climax of the story related to the development of Albert's character? (Analysis) *Answers will vary. Students should note that Albert's quick action during the fire and his response to his mother before he faints show that he has become his own person. (RL.6–10.3)*

4. The final section of the story summarizes the lives of the main characters after the fire. Based on this summary, what lifestyle do you think the narrator most favors: that of a be-er or a doer? Cite specific passages to support your answer. (Analysis) *Answers will vary. Most students will likely say be-er: When describing the place where her mother grew up, the narrator realizes that there is beauty there and that her mother was "in a hurry" and that she never "stopped long enough to take notice of things like that" (p. 44). (RL.6–12.1)*

Special Focus: Birth Order

Some believe that a person's birth order affects his or her personality. Have students study the following characteristics of the only, firstborn, middle, and last child. Do the characters in "Be-ers and Doers" match these descriptions? Ask students if they themselves match the descriptions.

Firstborn or Only Child: goal setting, high achieving, perfectionist, responsible, organized, rule keeping, determined, detail oriented

Middle Child: flexible, diplomatic, peacemaking, generous, social, competitive

Last Child: risk taking, outgoing, full of ideas, creative, funny, questioning of authority

Lists derived from these sources: *The Birth Order Challenge* by Clifford Isaacson; *The Birth Order Book* by Kevin Lehman.

Getting Ready by Debra Marquart, page 45

Prose Poem

Summary

A girl describes her daily morning panic of dressing for school and her family's reactions to her efforts.

Reading Hint	Thinking Skill	Extension
Because this poem is written in a modified stream-of-consciousness format, students may need help with the run-on sentences and unconventional punctuation.	Do girls and women experience this flurry of indecision about what to wear more than boys and men do?	**Compare/Contrast:** Have students compare and contrast the structure of the two poems "Getting Ready" and "The Changeling" (p. 32). *(RL.8.5)*

Vocabulary

cowlicks tufts of hair that stick out on the head

foraging searching for food; here it means rummaging

Discussing the Prose Poem

1. The girl calls herself the "thousand-change girl." Identify two passages from the poem that justify her name. (Recall) *". . . standing in my bedroom ripping pants and shirts from my body"; ". . . everything's in a pile on the floor." (RL.6–12.1)*

2. What title does the girl give her brother? (Recall) *She calls him "dressed-in-five-minutes."*

3. How do you think the girl feels about herself? (Analysis) *Answers will vary. She might feel insecure because she has a hard time figuring out what to wear. But in the end she feels that she looks good, so she seems confident. She also says that she doesn't care if her mom yells at her, so she's independent. Yet her difficulty in deciding what to wear might mean she's dependent on what's in style, and she has a need to fit in.*

4. How does the girl feel about the bus and the kids on it? Cite passages to support your answer. (Analysis) *Answers will vary. She doesn't seem too concerned about missing the bus. She hurries, but she also does not come downstairs until she is "looking good." She seems to treat getting*

ready as an art form. The other kids on the bus, by contrast, appear artless: "farm kids with cowlicks sitting in rows." (RL.6–12.1)

Language Focus: Compound Adjectives

Point out to students the compound adjectives the poet uses:

- *thousand-change* girl
- brother, *dressed-in-five-minutes*
- *great-lost-other* shoe

Have students create their own compound adjectives for some of the other people and objects in the poem. For example, they could describe the father, mother, farm kids, bus, and bedroom.

You could also have students create compound adjectives describing their own "Getting Ready." *(RL.6–12.4)*

How Do I Find Out Who I Am?

Critical Thinking Skill: DEFINING

1. Describe the character in the cluster with whom you most identified. Review the Concept Vocabulary on page 10 for words to use in your description. *Answers will vary. Accept any responses that students can justify. If students are having trouble identifying with a character, have them imagine sitting with one of the characters at lunch. What would they talk about?* (RL.6–12.4, RI.6–12.4)

2. In which story in the cluster does a parent have the most influence? Explain. *Answers will vary. Some students may claim that David's parents are instrumental in helping him work through school. Others may argue that the mother in "Be-ers and Doers" exerts the most control over her children.*

3. Using a chart such as the one below, rank how well the main character knows herself or himself by the end of the story, using the number 1 for "clueless" and 5 for "knowledgeable." Then provide a brief reason for your ranking. *Answers will vary. See the chart for possible answers.* (RL.6–12.1, RL.6–12.2, RI.6–12.1, RI.6–12.2)

Character	Ranking	Reason for Ranking
The prince in "Remember Me"	2	The prince has figured out who he used to be, but he doesn't want to find out who his wife-to-be really is.
David Raymond in "On Being Seventeen, Bright, and Unable to Read"	5	*David has a strong sense of himself and a good perspective due to the fact that he has overcome difficulties.*
The speaker in "The Changeling/ Transformación"	3	*She is confident enough to experiment with her identity. Still, she seems confused about her role as a young woman.*
The speaker in "Getting Ready"	4	*She knows how to have fun with her identity. She does seem a little worried about how other people will react.*
Albert in "Be-ers and Doers"	5	*He rebels against his mother's pressure to be a "doer." Now he seems completely comfortable with the life he has chosen.*

4. Pick a character from either "Remember Me," "The Changeling," or "Getting Ready," and explain why your character would agree or disagree with the following statement: "The clothes make the person." *Answers will vary. The prince would probably agree with the statement somewhat wryly. The girls in the poems would probably empathize with this quote.* (RL.6–12.2, RI.6–12.2)

Writing Activity: Defining Who You Are

The handout on the next page provides a graphic organizer to help students with the writing activity or use the interactive whiteboard lesson, WhoAmI_1.3_Writing. You may wish to use the Writing Activity Handout as an assessment. See also pages 62–64 for sample rubrics to use with student essays and projects. For a writing rubric to evaluate this activity, see the whiteboard lesson WhoAmI_1.4_CCSSRubric. *(W.6–12.4, W.6–12.5)*

Writing Activity: Defining Who You Are

Directions: Consider the story "Be-ers and Doers." Create your own definitions of the terms "be-er" and "doer" and write them in the chart below. Then decide whether you are a "be-er" or a "doer." Make a list of other words that define who you are and that end in *-er*. For example, you might be a "listener" or "music maker." Then in either prose or poetry, define yourself using the words you have chosen. Use the space under "Who I Am" to share your writing.

My definition of "be-er":
My definition of "doer":
-er words that define who I am:
Who I Am

Cluster One Vocabulary Test pages 12–45

Choose the meaning of the bold word in each passage.

1. "Let that be a lesson to you, you **arrogant** pig." (*"Remember Me," p. 13*)

   Ⓐ insecure Ⓒ overly proud
   Ⓑ aggressive Ⓓ obese

2. Going to the back of the building, I find my horse tied to a post, looking **disconsolate.** (*"Remember Me," p. 16*)

   Ⓐ extremely arrogant
   Ⓑ hopelessly unhappy
   Ⓒ incredibly hungry
   Ⓓ very angry

3. *But she didn't call me a frog,* I **console** myself . . . (*"Remember Me," p. 17*)

   Ⓐ tell Ⓒ comfort
   Ⓑ remind Ⓓ convince

4. PIN numbers and passwords have become strictly **passé.** (*"Your Body Is Your ID," p. 28*)

   Ⓐ required Ⓒ too expensive
   Ⓑ illegal Ⓓ out of date

5. . . . personal information can be easily **pilfered** by computer-savvy renegades and pranksters. (*"Your Body Is Your ID," p. 28*)

   Ⓐ enhanced Ⓒ degraded
   Ⓑ ridiculed Ⓓ stolen

6. I invented a game that made him look up / from his reading and shake his head / as if both **baffled** and amused. (*"The Changeling," p. 32*)

   Ⓐ eager Ⓒ reluctant
   Ⓑ confused Ⓓ anxious

7. Personal chemistry, I thought as I grew older, is a mysterious and **contrary** thing. (*"Be-ers and Doers," p. 38*)

   Ⓐ bizarre Ⓒ predictable
   Ⓑ dangerous Ⓓ contradictory

8. I was twenty-three now, and more interested in Albert than in **conformity.** (*"Be-ers and Doers," p. 39*)

   Ⓐ traveling Ⓒ independence
   Ⓑ careers Ⓓ obedience

9. He was sitting on the floor in his striped pajamas, holding Jennifer, rocking her, and singing songs to her in a low, **crooning** voice. (*"Be-ers and Doers," p. 41*)

   Ⓐ rasping Ⓒ serenading
   Ⓑ intimidating Ⓓ harsh

10. i'm kneeling in front of / the closet, **foraging** for that great-lost-other-shoe. (*"Getting Ready," p. 45*)

    Ⓐ rummaging Ⓒ praying
    Ⓑ hoping Ⓓ whining

CLUSTER TWO

Analyzing

I. Present this definition to students.

In **analyzing** you break down a topic or subject into parts so that it is easier to understand.

II. Discuss with students how they already use analysis by sharing the situations below.

You use analysis when you

- study the moves of an outstanding athlete
- pick out a new hairstyle or go shopping for new clothes
- learn the rules for a new game or learn how to use new software

You might invite students to suggest other situations where analysis would be used.

III. Explain to students that they will analyze the selections in Cluster Two to help answer the question "Where do I fit?"

A. Use the reproducible "What I Do to Fit In" on the next page as a blackline master or use the interactive whiteboard lesson, WhoAmI_2.1_CriticalThink.

B. Discuss with students the importance of fitting in and the methods people use to do so. Then have them fill out the worksheet as directed.

For additional in-depth work on developing the skill of analyzing, see the whiteboard lesson, WhoAmI_2.2_CCSSThinking. *(RL.6–12.1, RL.6–12.2, RL.6–12.3, RI.6–12.1, RI.6–12.2, RI.6–12.3)*

What I Do to Fit In

Cluster Question: Where do I fit?

Analyzing: Analyzing means to break a topic into parts so that it is easier to understand.

Directions: Most people want to feel like they fit in. It is uncomfortable to feel too different or to be rejected by those around us. To make matters even more complicated, we have to adjust to different environments or situations: life at home, at school, with friends, or at work. For each of the places listed below, analyze what you do to fit in. For example, you might laugh at your father's jokes at home just to keep him happy. Finally, explain where you think it is most important to fit in.

What I do to fit in at home

What I do to fit in at school

What I do to fit in with friends

Place that I feel it is most important to fit in, and why

Cluster Two Vocabulary

Watch for the following words as you read the selections in Cluster Two. Record your own vocabulary words and definitions on the blank lines.

Tiffany, age eleven pages 48–51

defensive resisting attack; protective

diverse varied; here it means composed of different ethnic groups or classes

exploited selfishly used for profit or gain

presume assume; suppose; take for granted

_____

_____

_____

The Green Killer pages 52–57

disdain hatred; contempt; scorn

enthralled captivated; charmed

flaunted paraded; boldly displayed

gala special; festive

_____

_____

_____

The Cutting of My Long Hair pages 58–61

anguish extreme distress; suffering or pain

immodestly indecently; shamelessly

venture try something risky or dangerous

_____

_____

_____

The Way Up pages 62–72

cowering crouching in fear or shame

decrepit weak from old age; feeble; infirm

exclusive friendly with few if any people; extremely private

hefted lifted; hoisted

loafing lounging lazily or idly

methodically systematically; in an organized way

resentful full of annoyance; bitter

sufficient adequate; enough

wheezed breathed with difficulty; made a whistling sound while breathing

_____

_____

_____

_____

Tiffany, age eleven as told to Rebecca Carroll, pages 48–51 Personal Essay

Summary

Tiffany, a young African American girl, frankly shares her feelings about several topics, including black and white relations, rap music, and her life at home and school.

Reading Hint	Thinking Skill	Extension
Because this essay evolved from an interview, it has a conversational style. Each paragraph has a specific focus that can be examined.	Why do you think Tiffany has such a positive self-image?	**Writing Activity:** Have students come up with a list of ten adjectives that describe who Tiffany is. *(RI.6–12.4)*

Vocabulary

defensive resisting attack; protective

diverse varied; here it means composed of different ethnic groups or classes

exploited selfishly used for profit or gain

presume assume; suppose; take for granted

Discussing the Personal Essay

1. How does Tiffany describe the members of her family? Cite passages from the story to support you answer. (Recall) *Tiffany describes her mother as caring but not so caring as to "lose sight of herself." Tiffany describes her father as "weird" in that he is "not afraid to do anything at all. . . . he is . . . fearless." Tiffany has difficulty describing her brother since he is under a lot of pressure to appear "tough and cool." (RI.6–12.1)*

2. Why does Tiffany wish there were black teachers at her school? (Recall) *She feels that the black students need black teachers as role models. It bothers her that there are black custodians and not black teachers.*

3. What do you think Tiffany means when she says there is a difference between "close" and "real close"? (Analysis) *Answers will vary. Some people you feel you can tell anything to. People of the same race share more with each other and understand each other better.*

4. What kind of future do you think Tiffany will have? (Analysis) *Answers will vary. She is confident and thoughtful, so she will probably have a bright future. She seems focused and imaginative. Her many friends*

indicate that she will probably get along well with others. She wants to do something that leads to discovery and inventions, so she will probably have an interesting career.

Special Focus: The Interview

After students have read this selection, have them interview each other about the topic of identity. Here are some simple steps students can follow to conduct their interviews. *(SL.6–12.1)*

1. Schedule an interview time.

2. Prepare 5–10 questions to ask, such as the following. (Notice that these questions require more than simple Yes/No responses.)
   - How do you feel about your identity?
   - What are your main interests?
   - How do your friends influence who you are?
   - How does your family influence your identity?
   - How important is it to you to fit in?

3. Ask the interviewee for permission to use a tape recorder if you plan to use one.

4. Transcribe, or write out, important parts of your interview to share with the class.

Discussing the Image

Do you think the illustration complements Tiffany's comments? Why or why not?

The Green Killer by M. E. Kerr, pages 52–57 Short Story

Summary

Alan Dunn relives his sixteenth year, when Blaze, his popular, rich, and successful cousin suddenly dies. After the death, Alan takes on his cousin's identity—wearing his clothes and even passing off one of Blaze's papers as his own. However, Alan is unable to live up to his cousin's killer instincts.

Reading Hint	Thinking Skill	Extension
"The Green Killer" refers to both the praying mantis and the emotion of jealousy.	How does jealousy affect Alan's actions?	**The Green Killer:** Discuss with students the similarities between the paper, the insect, and jealousy.

Vocabulary

disdain hatred; contempt; scorn

enthralled captivated; charmed

flaunted paraded; boldly displayed

gala special; festive

Discussing the Short Story

1. Why does Alan feel inferior to Blaze? (Recall) *Blaze is better looking and a better student. His family has more money, and he has an exotic name.*

2. What happens when Alan begins to wear Blaze's clothing? Cite passages from the story to support your answer. (Recall) *Alan begins to feel more confident. As evidence, Mr. Van Fleet notes, "You've changed, Alan. I don't mean just this essay—but you." Also, Courtney Sweet waits for Alan by his locker, "purring her congratulations." (RL.6–12.1)*

3. Why do you think Blaze steals trivial objects from other people? (Analysis) *Answers will vary. Some may say that stealing gives him a thrill. Others may note that steals parts of other people's identities in order to create his own.*

4. M. E. Kerr chose to tell the story from Alan's point of view. What is the effect of this choice? (Analysis) *Answers will vary. The reader identifies with Alan and experiences his emotions—his distrust and jealousy of Blaze as well as his short-lived success. The reader is also able to listen in as Alan carries on a dialogue (in italics) with his dead cousin. (RL.6–8.6, RL.11–12.6)*

Special Focus: Pretense and Identity

After Alan turns in "The Green Killer" as his own paper, he thinks that he is finally getting the kind of attention he deserves. His pretense is discovered, however, and his "true," identity is revealed. Use the following questions to prompt discussion about issues related to pretense and identity.

- What happens when you pretend to be someone you are not?
- Can people learn something about themselves by pretending to be someone else?
- Is the process of adulating a person such as a famous rock star, athlete, or actor the same as pretending to be that person? Why or why not?

Special Focus: Irony

Explain to students the definition of irony: that reality is revealed to be different from appearance. Discuss the levels of irony in the story. *(RL.8.6, RL.11–12.6, SL.6–12.1)*

- Alan takes Blaze at face value—that he was "brilliant, dazzling, a straight-A student" only to find out that Blaze had constructed a fake identity just as Alan tries to do.
- The title of the paper describes not only the praying mantis but the emotion that "kills" the new Alan.
- The irony adds humor as well as certain poetic justice.

The Cutting of My Long Hair by Zitkala-Ša, pages 58–61   Personal Essay

Summary

Zitkala-Ša, a young Dakota Sioux girl, recalls her first traumatic day at a Quaker missionary school. Despite her protest, the missionaries cut her long hair in order to "Americanize" her.

Reading Hint	Thinking Skill	Extension
Have students guess at the meaning of footnoted terms before reading the footnotes.	Why did the missionaries feel the need to change the way the Sioux children dressed and looked?	**Venn Diagram:** With the class create and discuss a Venn Diagrams highlighting the differences and similarities between Zitkala-Ša's native culture and the culture of the mission school.

Vocabulary

anguish extreme distress; suffering or pain

immodestly indecently; shamelessly

venture try something risky or dangerous

Discussing the Personal Essay

1. Why does Zitkala-Ša cry when she is in the dining room? (Recall) *She is upset and confused about when to sit or stand. Her confusion makes her "afraid to venture anything more."*

2. Why is it so important to Zitkala-Ša that she struggle against the missionaries, even though her struggle is futile? (Analysis) *Answers will vary. Her own culture is shamed by tight-fitting clothes and shingled hair. If she struggles, she will feel less ashamed when she is finally made to give in to the missionaries' demands.*

3. Why does Zitkala-Ša mention her mother repeatedly? (Analysis) *Answers will vary. She is still a child and needs her mother in this time of trauma. Her mother would understand her shame and would try to rescue her.*

4. What might be the author's purpose for writing this memoir? (Analysis) *Answers will vary. She might wish to preserve the memory of her culture. She might wish to let her ancestors know that she resisted the humiliation she was made to suffer.* (RI.6–12.6)

Historical Focus: Sioux Indians

From first contact, there was misunderstanding and conflict between Native American and European cultures. As Europeans overran Native American lands, they set up mission schools such as the one depicted here in order to replace the native identity with European values.

Zitkala-Ša's long hair and modest clothing were important parts of her cultural identity. Taking them away was part of an attempt to destroy Native American cultures. Discuss with students other ways in which identity can be robbed from a group of people, such as prohibiting them from practicing their religion or speaking their language.

Discussing the Image

The doll on page 58 is like one that Zitkala-Ša would have played with as a young girl. Do you think missionaries would allow her to keep such a doll? Why or why not?

In what ways is Zitkala-Ša like a doll in the hands of the missionaries? (RI.6–12.7)

Comparing Texts

Have students compare and contrast the sense of the author's identity as it comes through in this memoir with the brief biography of her by Roseanne Hoefel, which can be found online. (RI.6.9)

The Way Up by William Hoffman, pages 62–72

Short Story

Summary

Jamie, who is about to graduate, fears that no one will remember him after high school. To make his mark, he climbs a water tower and leaves evidence of his climb.

Reading Hint	Thinking Skill	Extension
What Jamie attempted was dangerous and could have been fatal. It is vital to defuse thoughts of heroism or a desire to replicate Jamie's actions.	Why do you think Jamie created his plan in such elaborate detail?	**Discussion:** Have students complete the story by telling what happens to Jamie the day after his dangerous climb.

Vocabulary

cowering crouching in fear or shame

decrepit weak from old age; feeble; infirm

exclusive friendly with few if any people; extremely private

hefted lifted; hoisted

loafing lounging lazily or idly

methodically systematically; in an organized way

resentful full of annoyance; bitter

sufficient adequate; enough

wheezed breathed with difficulty; made a whistling sound while breathing

Discussing the Short Story

1. How can we tell that Jamie is intelligent? (Recall) *He plans his climb thoroughly, buying the proper tools and waiting for the right weather. He carefully escapes from his house.*

2. Cite the passage in which Jamie becomes motivated to risk the climb. (Analysis) *Students should cite the statements about Jamie made by Nick and Alf when looking at the yearbook: "Not even the Glee Club" and "They'll never know you been here" (p. 63).* (RL.6–12.1)

3. What do you think would have happened if Jamie had tied the bandanna to the railing and climbed down without reaching the top of the tower? (Analysis) *Answers will vary. He probably would have felt that he failed.*

4. What did Jamie accomplish by climbing the tower? (Analysis) *Answers will vary. Most students will point out that Jamie proved his manhood to himself.*

Literary Focus: Suspense

Writers usually don't want to give away an exciting ending. They want to withhold the ending in order to build suspense and keep readers on the edge of their seats.

One of the key ingredients to writing suspense is detail. In "The Way Up," William Hoffman goes into great detail about Jamie's climb, creating a play-by-play feel to Jamie's dangerous adventure. Each step contains its own danger, thus increasing the suspense with each page.

Ask students to find and read aloud passages that heighten the suspense. (RL.6.5, RL.9–12.5, SL.6–12.1)

Saying Yes by Diana Chang, page 73

Poem

Summary

A Chinese American girl shares her confusion about her identity. She feels torn between her Chinese ancestry and her American reality. But most of all, she is weary of explaining her dual heritage.

Reading Hint	Thinking Skill	Extension
Students may be confused by the dialogue in the poem. Help them identify the two voices.	How does the poet's name relate to the poem itself?	**Dialogue Poem:** Have students write a poem or narrative in the same format as "Saying Yes" that speaks to their own different selves. *(W.6–12.3)*

Vocabulary

No vocabulary words

Discussing the Poem

1. What is the national or cultural identity of the speaker? (Recall) *She is Chinese American.*

2. Why does she want to say yes twice? (Recall) *She wants to say yes to being a Chinese American, rather than being just Chinese or just American. (RL.6–12.1)*

3. Why does she mention the homes she has had? (Analysis) *Answers will vary. People ask her to explain or justify her cultural identity, so she ends up explaining her past in more detail than she would like. She has lived in both China and the United States. People are curious about her past because of her cultural heritage.*

4. How do you think the poet feels when she is asked about her cultural identity? (Analysis) *Answers will vary. She might be tired of people asking her if she is Chinese or American. She might be tired of explaining that she considers herself to be both. She seems proud of that but also frustrated that it isn't easy to explain or accept.*

Special Focus: How Does Culture Influence Identity?

Discuss with students how most people gain a large share of their identity from their culture. The religion they practice, the food they eat, their sense of humor, and how much they value money or education can, at least in part, be traced to cultural influences. Use the following questions to discuss the relationship between culture and identity.

- What aspects of life might cause tension for a young person who lives in two cultures? *Dating expectations might be different. It may be hard to communicate with older generations due to language differences.*
- Do you think it is possible to create an identity outside your culture?
- Do you think cultural influences are good, or do you think such influences should be resisted? Explain.

Where Do I Fit?

Critical Thinking Skill: ANALYZING

1. Tiffany makes a number of strong statements in the first selection. Choose one of her statements and explain why you agree or disagree. *Answers will vary. Accept any responses students can justify. (W.6–12.1, W.6–12.2)*

2. Rank how much each of the following characters cares about fitting in and analyze why. Finally, rank yourself. Use a scale from *1* to *5*, with *1* as "not caring at all" and *5* as "caring a great deal." *Answers will vary. See chart below for sample responses.*

Character	Ranking	Reason for Ranking
Tiffany	1	She is not afraid to express unpopular feelings.
Alan	5	He is willing to give up his own identity in order to fit in.
Zitkala-Ša	3	She resists white culture, but she longs to return to her native culture.
Jamie	5	He is willing to risk his life to fit in and be more respected by his peers.
Myself		Answers will vary.

3. Pretend you're a talk show host who has invited a character from one of the stories to your show. Make up two questions you would ask that person, and write what you think his or her responses would be. *Answers will vary.*

4. Using the dialogue format of "Saying Yes" as your guide, write a poem about fitting in. The subject of the poem may be either you or a character from one of the stories. *Answers will vary.*

5. What is Jamie trying to achieve by climbing the tower in the story "The Way Up"? *Answers will vary. Some may note that Jamie is trying to achieve peer recognition and notoriety. Others may believe that he wants to prove to himself that he is someone who will be remembered.* In your opinion, does he achieve it? *Most will probably agree that he achieves his goal.*

6. Take the chart on self-knowledge that you started in Cluster 1 and rank the self-knowledge of the characters in this cluster. *Answers will vary. Accept responses that students can justify. See sample responses to question 2 above for character names.*

Writing Activity: Analyzing the Importance of Fitting In

The handout on page 36 provides a graphic organizer to help students with the writing activity or use the interactive whiteboard lesson, WhoAmI_2.3_Writing. You may wish to use the Writing Activity Handout as an assessment. See also pages 62–64 for sample rubrics to use with student essays and projects. For a writing rubric to evaluate this activity, see the whiteboard lesson WhoAmI_2.4_CCSSRubric. *(RL.6–12.1, RL.8.3, W.6–12.2)*

Writing Activity: Analyzing the Importance of Fitting In

Directions: In most of the selections in this cluster, the main characters weigh the pros and cons of fitting in. Analyze the changes these characters make or refuse to make. Write a short essay entitled "Fitting in Means . . ." Use examples from the stories to support your essay.

Use the chart below to help you organize examples from the selections in the cluster to use in your essay. First, find two or three quotations from the selections that show characters struggling with the issue of fitting in. Then comment on what the quotation says about the topic. Use your strongest quotations and comments in your essay.

Quotation	This example shows that fitting in means . . .
He had gone through four years of high school without leaving a mark. —Jamie in "The Way Up"	making a difference where you are—perhaps so that the place is different because you were there

Remember, a strong analysis

- states the purpose of the analysis
- demonstrates careful examination of each part of the topic
- supports each point with evidence
- ends with a summary of the ideas presented

Cluster Two Vocabulary Test pages 48–72

Choose the meaning of the bold word in each passage.

1. . . . I'm going to **presume** that it is not my responsibility to educate them in any sort of detail. (*"Tiffany, age eleven," p. 48*)

   Ⓐ assume   Ⓒ rely on
   Ⓑ determine   Ⓓ discount

2. I'm not **defensive** about the music I listen to and I don't really have a theory about it. (*"Tiffany, age eleven," p. 49*)

   Ⓐ picky   Ⓒ decisive
   Ⓑ protective   Ⓓ opinionated

3. . . . I really don't understand why any woman would actually agree to be in his videos knowing that they're going to be **exploited** like they are. (*"Tiffany, age eleven," p. 49*)

   Ⓐ ridiculed   Ⓒ used
   Ⓑ cheated   Ⓓ damaged

4. "He has everything . . . *everything*," my father added with a slight tone of **disdain,** for we all knew how spoiled my cousin was. (*"The Green Killer," p. 53*)

   Ⓐ respect   Ⓒ wisdom
   Ⓑ envy   Ⓓ scorn

5. . . . my cousin **flaunted** his riches before me with glee. (*"The Green Killer," p. 54*)

   Ⓐ paraded   Ⓒ abused
   Ⓑ destroyed   Ⓓ utilized

6. In my **anguish** I moaned for my mother, but no one came to comfort me. (*"The Cutting of My Long Hair," p. 61*)

   Ⓐ anxiety   Ⓒ pain
   Ⓑ anticipation   Ⓓ anger

7. At first he was **resentful** and hurt, as if betrayed. (*"The Way Up," p. 64*)

   Ⓐ surprised   Ⓒ bitter
   Ⓑ jealous   Ⓓ motivated

8. Occasionally a light wind gusted against his face and chest—not hard enough to worry him, but **sufficient** to slow his step. (*"The Way Up," p. 68*)

   Ⓐ not adequate   Ⓒ designed
   Ⓑ enough   Ⓓ determined

9. He **hefted** the anchor and with a gentle, looping motion arched it over himself. (*"The Way Up," p. 70*)

   Ⓐ grasped   Ⓒ dropped
   Ⓑ lifted   Ⓓ touched

10. As if **decrepit,** he shifted his weight onto the ladder. (*"The Way Up," p. 72*)

    Ⓐ afraid   Ⓒ hurried
    Ⓑ feeble   Ⓓ determined

CLUSTER THREE

Evaluating

I. Present this definition to students.

Evaluating is the process of making a judgment based on information, standards, or criteria.

II. Discuss with students how they already use evaluation by sharing the situations below.

You use evaluation when you
- choose which movie you want to see
- decide whether a move is legal according to the rules of a game
- decide whether you want to be friends with someone

You might invite students to suggest other situations where evaluation is used.

III. Explain to students that they will be creating a list of strong and weak qualities that they will use to evaluate the characters from the selections in Cluster Three. Use the following steps to show students how to evaluate.

A. Use the reproducible "Evaluating Character" on the next page as a blackline master or use the interactive whiteboard lesson, WhoAmI_3.1_CriticalThink.

B. Tell students to fill out the chart with qualities of strong and weak characters. Discuss their answers as a class.

C. Tell students to add to their lists as they read the selections in the cluster.
(RL.6–12.1, RI.6–12.1)

For additional in-depth work on developing the skill of evaluating, see the interactive whiteboard lesson, WhoAmI_3.2_CCSSThinking.
(RL.6–12.1, RL.6–12.2, RL.6–12.3, RI.6–12.1, RI.6–12.2, RI.6–12.3)

Evaluating Character

Cluster Question: What do I believe?

Evaluating: When **evaluating,** you make a judgment based on information, standards, or criteria.

Directions: When people refer to a person's character, they are referring to that person's willingness to live up to what he or she believes in. For example, a person who *says* she believes in helping others might ride her bicycle past the scene of an accident without stopping because a friend is waiting for her at home. Such a person is more concerned about her own affairs than the needs of others.

How do you judge a person's character? First, you need a set of standards against which to compare the person's actions or qualities. Complete the chart below by writing at least six actions or qualities of people with strong and weak characters. Use the lists to judge the characters in the selections in this cluster. Feel free to add to your standards list if a character in one of the selections reveals a particularly strong or weak characteristic. Remember, the best way to see a person's true character is when that person is tested in some way.

A person with a strong character	A person with a weak character
Thinks of others	*Ignores the needs of others*

Cluster Three Vocabulary

Watch for the following words as you read the selections in Cluster Three. Record your own vocabulary words and definitions on the blank lines.

Born Worker pages 76–85

array a large number or quantity

cooed murmured softly; gave comfort

retort a sharp, witty, or severe reply

stagnant foul and stale from sitting; not flowing

trappings ornamental articles of dress or equipment

_____

_____

_____

Dolly's False Legacy pages 86–89

intrusion the act of bringing in without invitation or permission; invasion

morality rightness; ethics

render make; demonstrate; show

_____

_____

_____

Moon pages 90–108

demeanor conduct; behavior; deportment

disquiet anxiety; uneasiness; lack of calm

illumined lit up; made clear or lucid

ominous threatening; predicting evil or harm; foreboding

pandemonium uproar; chaos; tumult

sullen showing ill humor, gloomy

_____

_____

_____

I'm Nobody page 109

bog wet and spongy ground; marsh

_____

_____

_____

Born Worker by Gary Soto, pages 76–85

Short Story

Summary

José, from a working-class family, is approached by his wealthier cousin Arnie, who wants to form a company in order to earn money. Predictably, Arnie wants to be the brains of the outfit, and he wants José to do all the work. Arnie settles for 30 percent of the income after José refuses to work for anything less. The cousins' true characters are revealed when a client hurts himself. José acts immediately to aid the client while Arnie runs away.

Reading Hint	Thinking Skill	Extension
The story begins abruptly and readers may not understand at first who "they" are. Have them look for clues in context.	How might you account for the difference between José's character and Arnie's character?	**Future Lives:** Have students write a paragraph in which they compare what the two cousins will be like as adults. (W.6–12.2)

Vocabulary

array a large number or quantity

cooed murmured softly; gave comfort

retort a sharp, witty, or severe reply

stagnant foul and stale from sitting; not flowing

trappings ornamental articles of dress or equipment

Discussing the Short Story

1. What is the business arrangement between Arnie and José? (Recall) *José earns 70 percent of the money and does almost all the labor. Arnie helps out with the labor, books the jobs, and earns 30 percent.*

2. What is the difference between Arnie's family and José's family? (Recall) *Arnie's family is middle class and has money for exotic vacations. Jose's family is working class. They do not have money for fancy vacations and expensive clothes.*

3. Why does José climb the telephone pole? (Analysis) *Answers will vary. José wants to escape his cousin's lying and jabbering. He also wants to see the world from his father's perspective, a perspective that honors honesty and hard work. (RL.6–12.1)*

4. What is the theme of the story? Cite specific details from the story to support your answer. (Analysis) *Answers will vary.*

Theme: Deeds speak louder than words. Hard work is its own reward. José sees himself from the perspective of his father and knows that he would see a "good worker . . . and a good man" (p. 85). (RL.6–12.2)

Special Focus: Character

Authors use dialogue to reveal character. With your students discuss verbal exchanges that show the character differences between Arnie and José. In this exchange on page 78, Arnie shows his laziness and José reveals his directness and honesty.

"What would you do?" José asked.
"Me?" he said brightly. "Shoot, I'll round up all kinds of jobs for you. You won't have to do anything." He stopped, then started again. "Except—you know—do the work."
"Get out of here," José said.

Ask students to find two other exchanges of dialogue that reveal these characters. (RL.6–7.5, RL.11–12.5)

Comparing Media

Show students the student-made video dramatization of "Born Worker" on YouTube and have them compare and contrast the experience of reading the story and viewing the video. Also ask them to consider how faithful the dramatization is to the original. (RL.6–8.7)

Dolly's False Legacy by Ian Wilmut, pages 86–89
Essay

Summary

The scientist in charge of creating Dolly, the famous cloned sheep, discusses the moral implications of his landmark accomplishment.

Reading Hint	Thinking Skill	Extension
This essay was written for adults. Students might find the syntax confusing or intimidating. Stop frequently to discuss the essay in order to make it more accessible to all students.	With students list the pros and cons of cloning according to Ian Wilmut.	**Writing Exercise:** Have students make a two-column chart. Ask them to imagine they have a clone. In one column, have them list everything in a typical day they would still do themselves. In the other, have them list what they would delegate to their clones. If they could have a clone, how would their lives change? Would it be a good idea to have a clone who would function as a slave? (W.6–12.2)

Vocabulary

intrusion the act of bringing in without invitation or permission; invasion

morality rightness; ethics

render make; demonstrate; show

Discussing the Essay

1. According to the essay, how does human personality emerge? (Recall) *It emerges from a combination of nature and nurture—partly things we inherit and partly our environment.*

2. Why does the author think it is wrong to try to copy a child? (Recall) *He thinks each child should be wanted for himself or herself. If a dead child is cloned, then the clone will be expected to replace the original, depriving the clone of individuality.* (RI.6–12.1, RI.6–10.8)

3. Why do you think Dr. Wilmut cloned a sheep when he is aware of the dangers of cloning? (Analysis) *Answers will vary. He thinks cloning can produce important scientific and medical discoveries.*

4. What issues should laws about cloning address? (Analysis) *Answers will vary. Among issues students may mention are whether people should be cloned and, if so, under what circumstances cloning should be allowed.*

Special Focus: Nature vs. Nurture

Ian Wilmut notes that the human personality "emerges from both the effects of the genes we inherit (nature) and environmental factors (nurture)." The debate over which is more important, nature or nurture, has engaged philosophers and scientists for centuries. Use the following questions to open a discussion on the topic of nature vs. nurture. (SL.6–12.1)

- Some scientists have put forth the theory that certain aspects of personality may be genetic, such as the propensity to commit acts of violence. What implications might this theory have on the notion that people should be held responsible for their actions?

- If you were going to adopt a child, would it be important to you that the birth parents had particular physical and intellectual characteristics? For example, would race, IQ, or athletic ability matter to you?

Analyzing Structure

Help students through a paragraph-by-paragraph analysis of the structure of this essay. For each major section, ask students to explain its importance to the whole. Also help students focus on the structure of one paragraph, explaining how certain sentences convey key ideas. (RI.7–10.5)

Moon by Chaim Potok, pages 90–108

Short Story

Summary

Moon, a 13-year-old boy, has one passion—drumming. He also has a hard time controlling his anger against his parents and the world. His world view is enlarged through a brief meeting with Ashraf, a child laborer from Pakistan who also shares a talent for drumming. When Ashraf is assassinated for campaigning against child labor, Moon performs an empassioned drum solo that opens his parents' eyes to his talent and provides a creative outlet for his anger.

Reading Hint	Thinking Skill	Extension
This short story is fairly long. The reading may need to be divided into two sittings.	Why was Ashraf assassinated?	**Compare and Contrast:** With students, make a Venn diagram comparing and contrasting Moon and Ashraf. Discuss. *(SL.6–12.1)*

Vocabulary

demeanor conduct; behavior; deportment

disquiet anxiety; uneasiness; lack of calm

illumined lit up; made clear or lucid;

ominous threatening; predicting evil or harm; foreboding

pandemonium uproar; chaos; tumult

sullen showing ill humor, gloomy

Discussing the Short Story

1. How can you tell that Moon is truly committed to drumming? (Recall) *He knows a great deal of technical information about it and has memorized the works of famous drummers. He gets joy from practicing.*

2. How does Moon feel about Ashraf when he sees him at school? Support your answer with specific details from the text. (Recall) *He is fascinated by him. He wants his friend to be quiet so he can concentrate on Ashraf's drumming. (RL.6–12.1)*

3. How do you think Moon's life will change after his drum solo? (Analysis) *Answers will vary. His parents seem to recognize his passion for drumming. It may be easier for him to build the recording studio. He may become less self-absorbed and angry, and more concerned with others' problems.*

Special Focus: Child Labor and Identity

Make students aware that in the United States today, there are laws that prohibit children from working until they reach a certain age. Once they can legally work, there are laws guaranteeing them a minimum wage for their labor and limiting the number of hours they can work. These laws came about to make sure that children were protected from the exploitation that Ashraf endured. Use the following questions to open a discussion on the relationship between child labor and identity. *(SL.6–12.1)*

- Do you think that the system of child labor that exists in some countries keeps young people from finding their true identities?
- How much do you think the work you do defines you?
- Do you think that the system of education in the United States ensures that young people can discover and develop their talents? Why or why not?

I'm Nobody by Emily Dickinson, page 109

Poem

Summary

In this famous poem, the speaker speculates on the pleasures and wisdom of anonymity.

Reading Hint	Thinking Skill	Extension
Dickinson's style, which includes many dashes and unconventional capitalization, may bewilder students. You might have students look for the natural sentence breaks.	In what ways is a frog public?	**Identity Poem:** Have students write a poem about themselves in similar format to "I'm Nobody."

Vocabulary

bog wet and spongy ground; marsh

Discussing the Poem

1. Who does the speaker think she is? (Recall) *She thinks she is nobody.*

2. Why doesn't the speaker want people to advertise that there are two nobodies? (Recall) *She is afraid that it will attract attention. (RL.6–12.1)*

3. Why do you think the speaker wants to be private? (Analysis) *Answers will vary. She seems to think it would take a lot of her time if she were public. It would get old and dreary to have to talk to people. She has better things to do.*

4. What do you think the poet thinks of herself? (Analysis) *Answers will vary. She seems to have good self-esteem. She likes herself the way she is and doesn't feel pressured to fit in or be liked. She wants to be alone.*

5. What is the structure of the poem, and how does it contribute to the poem's meaning? (Analysis) *The first stanza focuses on "nobody-ness." The second stanza, using parallel rhythms, focuses on "somebody-ness." The separation of the two ideas reinforces the idea of privacy that comes with being a nobody. (RL.6–12.5)*

Discussing the Image

What insight does this photograph give into Dickinson's words?

Special Focus:
Public vs. Private Identities

As a reader might guess from the poem, Emily Dickinson was a fiercely private person. So private, in fact, that she seldom left her own house. She did not begin to gain recognition as a major American poet until after her death.

Use the following questions to discuss with students the differences between our private and public selves.

- Do you act differently at home than you do in public? Explain.

- Do you share a different part of yourself with your friends than you do with your family?

- Do you have a private part of yourself that you share with no one?

- Do you think fame and recognition can harm a person's sense of identity? Why or why not?

- Which do you think would be better— fame and recognition during life or after death?

What Do I Believe?

Critical Thinking Skill: EVALUATING

1. "Dolly's False Legacy" examines the issue of human cloning. List three pros and cons of cloning to help evaluate what you believe about this issue. Then tell what your opinion is. *(RI.6–10.8)*

2. Decide whether the speaker in "I'm Nobody" has self-confidence. Explain your response. *Answers will vary. Some may say that the speaker has self-confidence because he or she is not concerned with being noticed by others. Some may feel that the speaker seeks privacy because he or she is afraid or timid.*

3. Use the chart below to evaluate whether the characters in this cluster see themselves as "somebodies" or "nobodies," and whether you think they are "somebodies" or "nobodies." Be prepared to explain your responses. *Answers may vary. Students are likely to agree with the following assessments.*

Character	Sees self as	You see character as
José in "Born Worker"	somebody	somebody
Arnie in "Born Worker"	somebody	nobody
Ashraf in "Moon"	somebody	somebody

4. If you had to choose a subtitle for "Moon" that expresses the story's main idea, or theme, would it be "Moon: A Boy Learns to Control His Anger"; "Moon: Music Is a Universal Language"; or "Moon: Tragedy Forces Boy to Care About Others"? Explain your choice. If you don't think any of the choices states the main theme, write your own subtitle and explain why you think it expresses the main idea of the story. *Answers will vary. Accept responses that students can justify. If students are having trouble with this exercise, recap the story with them, highlighting the moments that pertain to the possible titles. (RL.6–12.2)*

5. Sometimes it takes a test or crisis to find out what you believe. What crises face José in "Born Worker" and Moon in "Moon"? Explain in a short paragraph what these tests teach the characters about what they believe. *Answers will vary. The following are some possible responses. José faces and deals with the injured man in the swimming pool. He learns that he believes in trust and honesty, and facing issues rather than running away like his cousin does. Moon faces a crisis when he learns that Ashraf was murdered for political reasons. He learns to channel his anger into his music.*

6. Take the chart on self-knowledge that you started in Cluster 1 and rank the self-knowledge of the characters in this cluster. *Answers will vary. Accept responses that students can justify.*

Writing Activity: My Credo

The handout on page 46 provides a graphic organizer to help students with the writing activity or use the interactive whiteboard lesson, WhoAmI_3.3_Writing. You may wish to use the Writing Activity Handout as an assessment. See also pages 62–64 for sample rubrics to use with student essays and projects. For a writing rubric to evaluate this activity, see the whiteboard lesson WhoAmI_3.4_CCSSRubric. *(W.6–12.4, W.6–12.5)*

Writing Activity: My Credo

Directions: Religions and professions often publish credos, or creeds, that state their fundamental beliefs and the principles that guide their actions. For example, the following is the first principle of the American Medical Association's Code of Medical Ethics: "A physician shall be dedicated to providing competent medical service with compassion and respect for human dignity." Evaluate what you believe and then write a credo, or statement of belief, entitled "Suitable for Framing."

Use the following chart to help you develop your credo.

Crises or difficulties I have experienced:
What I learned from the difficulties I have lived through:
Cause(s) I would be willing to support:
My credo:

To create a credo
- brainstorm a list of your beliefs in four categories: family, school, community, and one category of your own choosing, such as friends, recreation, or religion
- narrow your list to three core beliefs
- find a compelling but simple way to state each belief
- combine the statements into a pleasing whole

Cluster Three Vocabulary Test pages 76–109

Choose the meaning of the bold word in each passage.

1. José thought a moment and said, "I'm not like you." He smiled at his **retort.** (*"Born Worker," p. 79*)

   Ⓐ witty reply   Ⓒ secret thought
   Ⓑ kind comment   Ⓓ hidden agenda

2. It leaped into the **stagnant** water with a plop. (*"Born Worker," pp. 83–84*)

   Ⓐ stale and foul   Ⓒ still and high
   Ⓑ still and chlorinated   Ⓓ turbulent and foul

3. Overlooked in the arguments about the **morality** of artificially reproducing life is the fact that, at present, cloning is a very inefficient procedure. (*"Dolly's False Legacy," p. 86*)

   Ⓐ practicality   Ⓒ ethics
   Ⓑ danger   Ⓓ opportunity

4. Couples unable to have children might choose to have a copy of one of them rather than accept the **intrusion** of genes from a donor. (*"Dolly's False Legacy," p. 87*)

   Ⓐ confusion   Ⓒ problem
   Ⓑ invasion   Ⓓ benefit

5. Inside Moon's mother, an unassuming woman of gentle **demeanor,** the picture of the gaunt, brown-faced Pakistani boy . . . abruptly winked out. (*"Moon," p. 92*)

   Ⓐ conduct   Ⓒ heritage
   Ⓑ thoughts   Ⓓ laughter

6. . . . the clamor erupting from the basement and streaming through the air ducts and filling the house with that booming drumming twanging **pandemonium** they call music. (*"Moon," p. 92*)

   Ⓐ volcano   Ⓒ concert
   Ⓑ uproar   Ⓓ assembly

7. Moon . . . had . . . run up to his room and slammed his door shut with such force that, to the **disquiet** of his father, the paint cracked near the ceiling on the hallway wall. (*"Moon," p. 94*)

   Ⓐ silence   Ⓒ anger
   Ⓑ shock   Ⓓ anxiety

8. And Morgan—so edgy and **sullen,** so fixed upon himself. (*"Moon," p. 94*)

   Ⓐ emotional   Ⓒ private
   Ⓑ gloomy   Ⓓ skinny

9. He would put a CD into the stereo player in the den, fill the air with swelling, pounding music that drove away the **ominous** silences . . . (*"Moon," p. 100*)

   Ⓐ lonesome   Ⓒ threatening
   Ⓑ long   Ⓓ demanding

10. Moon, slowly raising his head, saw his parents staring at him, their faces like suddenly **illumined** globes. (*"Moon," p. 108*)

    Ⓐ lit up   Ⓒ confused
    Ⓑ disturbed   Ⓓ hopeless

Teaching Cluster Four

The final cluster in *Who Am I?* can be presented using one or more of the following methods.
- presented by the teacher
- used for independent student learning
- used for a final assessment

Use the chart below, or the interactive whiteboard lesson, WhoAmI_4.0_Teaching, to plan.

Teacher Presentation	Independent Learning/Assessment
For teacher-directed study you can	**Students can**
• pass out cluster vocabulary sheet • set schedule for reading selections • use appropriate discussion questions and extension activities for each selection • administer vocabulary test • assign research projects • administer final essay test	• plan and present a lesson over one or more of the selections in the last cluster • prepare a vocabulary study sheet and create and administer a vocabulary test • conduct additional research on a related topic • respond to one or more of the questions or activities on the Responding to Cluster Four page

Teacher Notes

CLUSTER FOUR

Synthesizing and Integrating

I. Present this definition to students.

Synthesizing and **integrating** mean combining parts (facts, thoughts, or ideas) into a new whole.

II. Discuss with students how they already use synthesis/integration by sharing the situations below.

You use synthesis and integration when you

- use what you already know to figure out the meaning of a new word
- combine several brainstorming suggestions to develop a solution to a problem
- develop a consensus of opinion based upon everyone's ideas

Ask students to suggest other situations where synthesis and integration would be used.

III. Use the following steps to show students how to synthesize and integrate.

A. Use the reproducible "Who Might I Become?" on the next page as a blackline master or use the interactive whiteboard lesson, WhoAmI_4.1_CriticalThink.

B. Explain to students that they will use the handout to explore who they want to become. Have them fill in each area: Education and Occupation, Beliefs, Family Life, and Hobbies and Interests. Then have them write a character sketch on a separate sheet of paper that answers the question, "Who might I become?" You may want to complete a chart and character sketch for yourself to model the idea that we never stop becoming.

C. You might suggest that students revisit and update their chart periodically throughout their life. When can we say that we have finally *become?*

For additional in-depth work on developing the skills of synthesizing and integrating, see the whiteboard lesson WhoAmI_4.2_CCSSThinking. *(RL.6–12.2, RL.6–12.9)*

Who Might I Become?

Synthesizing: When **synthesizing,** you combine or rearrange statements, feelings, or ideas to provide a new or fresh perspective on a topic.

Directions: So far in this unit, you have defined, analyzed, and evaluated other characters. Now it is time for you to *synthesize* what you have learned by defining who *you* are. Fill in the chart below with traits and qualities of the person you want to become. For example, what occupation do you see yourself engaged in, and what education will it take to achieve that goal? Fill in the other areas as appropriate. When you have completed the chart, create a character sketch on a separate sheet of paper that answers the question, "Who might I become?"

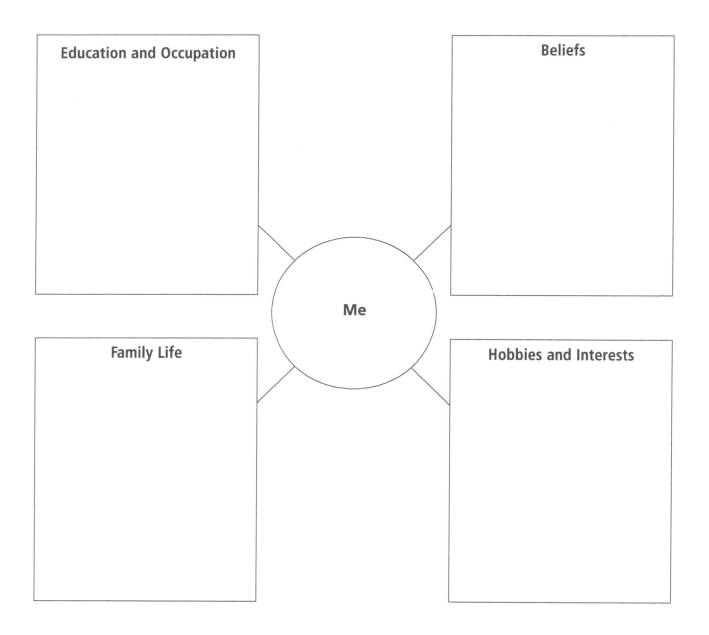

Education and Occupation

Beliefs

Me

Family Life

Hobbies and Interests

Cluster Four Vocabulary

Watch for the following words as you read the selections in Cluster Four. Record your own vocabulary words and definitions on the blank lines.

Fairy Tale pages 112–124

averting turning away; turning aside

cognizant aware; conscious

compulsive obsessive; following an irresistible impulse

lacrosse a team sport similar to soccer but with a smaller ball and sticks

manifested made clear; showed; was obvious

opulent wealthy; rich; affluent

prone inclined; tending toward; susceptible

skeptically doubtfully; hesitantly

snide negative in a nasty manner

taffeta an elegant fabric, usually stiff and shiny

_____

_____

_____

Fox Hunt pages 126–133

aristocrats people of noble background; people with taste and manners

decadent self-indulgent; decayed; declining

illustrious famous; widely respected; renowned

malicious vicious; hoping to cause injury

thatched made with leaves or straw

_____

_____

_____

Holly, age fifteen pages 134–137

heredity the handing down of genetic traits from parents to children

prestige dignity; good reputation

_____

_____

_____

Birthday Box pages 138–142

subtle indirect; delicate; in a manner difficult to perceive or understand

_____

_____

_____

Fairy Tale by Todd Strasser, pages 112–124

Short Story

Summary

This contemporary adaptation of Cinderella has many of the basic components of the original. In this version, however, Cynthia opts for an unconventional ending: she chooses the security of her own identity and a solid, honest friendship over everybody else's "prince charming."

Reading Hint	Thinking Skill	Extension
This story is set in New York City with many references to stores and places there.	Ask students to predict the conversation Cindy, Sheri, and Ruth might have after the dance.	**Character and Detail:** With students, review the scene in which Cynthia meets Sam in the cafeteria (p. 116) and list the details that reveal Sam's character. Decide as a class who Sam is. *(RL.6–12.3)*

Vocabulary

averting turning away; turning aside

cognizant aware; conscious

compulsive obsessive; following an irresistible impulse

lacrosse a team sport similar to soccer but with a smaller ball and sticks

manifested made clear; showed; was obvious

opulent wealthy; rich; affluent

prone inclined; tending toward; susceptible

skeptically doubtfully; hesitantly

snide negative in a nasty manner

taffeta an elegant fabric, usually stiff and shiny

Discussing the Short Story

1. What are Cynthia's mixed emotions about attending the cotillion? (Recall) *She is afraid to go, yet she wants to. She is upset with herself for caring if she fits in.*

2. List some details that foreshadow that Cynthia will decide to keep Sam's friendship rather than go with The One. (Analysis) *Students should note one or more of the following:*
• Cynthia and Sam share a sense of humor about, and are detached from, the social climbing scene.
• At the thrift store, Cynthia notices that Sam is good-looking.
• The One reveals a dull and shallow character when he asks Cynthia, "Wanna dance?" and when he starts talking about the things that reveal his family's wealth. (RL.6–8.6, RL.11–12.6)

3. What does Cynthia gain from going to the ball? (Analysis) *Answers will vary. She gains confidence with her peers because she makes such a good appearance, and she is rewarded with clarity when she realizes that her friendship with Sam is more important than popularity.*

Literary Focus: Flat and Round Characters

In most fiction, main characters tend to be *round* and minor characters tend to be *flat*. A round character is usually a main character whose identity readers get to know quite well through such details as his or her past history, likes and dislikes, physical characteristics, and dreams and goals. Flat characters, on the other hand, are not well drawn. Sometimes, they are even stereotypical.

Discuss with students which characters are flat and which are round in "Fairy Tale." *(SL.6–12.1)*

Discussing the Image

It could be said that the images that accompany this story are the stereotypical images of "the fairy-tale woman." How do you think Cynthia would feel about these images?

Side 32 by Victor Hernández Cruz, page 125   Poem

Summary

The speaker reacts to details of the urban landscape, rejecting some and embracing others.

Reading Hint	Thinking Skill	Extension
Encourage students to have fun with the unusual images in this poem.	What do you think is important to the speaker?	**I Am Glad:** Have students write a poem or short narrative using the same structure: "I am glad I am not . . ." or "I am glad I am . . ." *(W.6–12.3)*

Vocabulary

No vocabulary words

Discussing the Poem

1. What qualities do the things the speaker is glad he is not share; what qualities do the things he says he is share? Cite specific details to support your answer. (Analysis) *Answers will vary. The speaker is glad he is not trivial man-made objects that go unnoticed or are lost, such as a pipe in a factory or a lost subway token. The objects he identifies with are full of possibility and life, such as a man, a glass of water, a guitar string, and a butterfly.* (RL.6–12.1)

2. The speaker says, "I am nothing and no one / I am the possibility of everything." Consider the opposite idea. Does being "someone" mean that possibilities are limited? (Analysis) *Answers will vary. Some may agree that the more defined a person is, the fewer options they have to become someone different. Others may feel that becoming who you are allows for limitless growth.*

Literary Focus: An Image Is Worth a Thousand Words

Victor Hernández Cruz uses vivid details and imagery to convey the speaker's identity to the reader. Much like a photograph or painting, one or two clear images in a poem can tell more about a character than many paragraphs of prose.

Using images, photos, words, and phrases, have students create identity collages that tell the viewer/reader who they are.

Specific and General Details

Some of the details in the poem are very specific, such as the image of the subway token "by the edge of a building on 47th Street." Other details are more general, such as the statement, "I am nothing and no one." Discuss the impact of the different levels of detail in the poem.

Fox Hunt by Lensey Namioka, pages 126–133

Short Story

Summary

Andy, a Chinese American boy, is a "brain" who doesn't quite fit in. He meets a Lee, young Chinese American girl. Through their relationship as well as a fable about a fox that has been important to his father's identity, he gains the confidence to be himself.

Reading Hint	Thinking Skill	Extension
The third section of this story is a story-within-a-story, told by Andy's mother. Alert readers to the change of voice. This section is in italics.	Realistically, what reward do you think Lee is expecting?	**Discussion:** This story contrasts the value of hard work against the power of a magical fable—call it destiny. Discuss with the class the two sources of identity. Which is more important?

Vocabulary

aristocrats people of noble background; people with taste and manners

decadent self-indulgent; decayed; declining

illustrious famous; widely respected; renowned

malicious vicious; hoping to cause injury

thatched made with leaves or straw

Discussing the Short Story

1. Why does Andy's mother smile when Andy's father talks about their aristocratic ancestors? (Recall) *She smiles because she believes the real story is different from the one Andy's father presents.*

2. Why does Andy's father argue so vehemently against the story of the fox Andy's mother tells? Support your answer with details from the story. (Analysis) *Answers will vary. Andy's father has a lot of his identity wrapped up in the value of hard work and the family history of belonging to the mandarin class. As he says, "Liang Fujin passed the examinations because he was smart and worked hard" (p. 131).* (RL.6–12.1)

3. How does making friends with Lee affect Andy's self-image? (Analysis) *Answers will vary. He is amazed that an attractive, intelligent girl would befriend him, so he becomes more confident. She helps him with English, which makes him more confident*

about taking the PSAT. He also feels special because, as a fox, she has selected him in order to help him.

4. Fables often have a moral, or lesson. What do you think is the moral of the fable Andy's mother tells Andy? Support your answer with a detail from the story. (Analysis) *Answers will vary. The moral: hard work is rewarded. In the cases of both Andy and his ancestor Liang Fujin, both were willing to work hard and to endure loneliness to reach a goal.* (RL.6–12.2)

Special Focus: Create a Fable

A *fable* is a short tale that explains a moral lesson or natural phenomenon. Usually at least one of the central characters is an animal that possesses human characteristics. Have students follow these steps to create their own identity fables. (W.6–12.3)

- Select an issue on the topic of identity (e.g., the importance of remaining true to yourself).
- Choose animals and/or people who will be the main characters.
- Write the dialogue between the characters.
- Add an introduction and conclusion to the fable.

Holly, age fifteen as told to Jill Krementz, pages 134–137 Personal Essay

Summary

Holly shares the experience of discovering her birth mother and developing a relationship with her. Although her adoptive parents are supportive, the new relationship creates tension and challenges Holly to think about her identity.

Reading Hint	Thinking Skill	Extension
This narrative could evoke intense feelings in adopted students.	What questions would you want to ask Alison, the birth mother, if you were Holly?	Role-play a conversation between an adopted teenager and his or her birth parent. (SL.6–12.1)

Vocabulary

heredity the handing down of genetic traits from parents to children

prestige dignity; good reputation

Discussing the Personal Essay

1. How do the adults in Holly's life help her to cope with the shock of hearing from her birth mother? (Recall) *She feels close enough to the family friend to hug him and cry to him and tell him her story. Both parents are responsive to her. She can discuss things with them openly.*

2. What does Holly do after receiving the phone call? (Recall) *She has a family friend take her to find her parents.*

3. Why do you think Holly wanted to wait longer to find Alison? (Analysis) *Answers will vary. She wanted to wait until she was older and more mature, more able to deal with everyone's emotions.*

4. Why does Holly say that using her birth mother in arguments is something that cannot ever happen? (Analysis) *Answers will vary. She understands that hurtful things cannot always be taken back. She is afraid that invoking Alison's name when she and her mother are arguing will cause serious injury to their closeness as mother and daughter. (RI.6–12.1)*

Special Focus: Open Adoption

In generations past, adoption records were sealed or destroyed. Children were seldom told they were adopted, and those who were told did not necessarily have a way to contact their birth parents. The birth parents often did not know what became of their children.

In the latter part of the 20th century, women who gave their children up for adoption began demanding open adoption. This agreement, signed before the birth of the child, guarantees the birth mother the legal right to visit her child, and the child the right to know her as the birth mother.

Use the following questions to discuss these adoption rules with your students. (SL.6–12.1)

- What are some advantages to open adoption? *Knowing one's genetic heritage and health history helps determine susceptibility to diseases such as epilepsy, alcoholism, and depression, as well as an increased understanding of one's identity.*

- What are some complications to open adoption? *a more complicated family structure, conflict between parents*

- Which method of adoption is best for the parent? Which method is best for the child? *Answers will vary.*

Birthday Box by Jane Yolen, pages 138–142

Short Story

Summary

Teenager Katie remembers the death of her mother and her mother's mysterious last gift to her—an empty box. Her initial puzzlement over the gift and her anger about her mother's death evolve into speculation and, finally, into an understanding of the legacy her mother left for her—a gentle reminder to develop a strong sense of herself.

Reading Hint	Thinking Skill	Extension
Explain to students that although the story begins with an incident that occurred when the narrator was ten, she is now a teenager telling the story in the form of a flashback.	What does the gift Katie receives tell readers about Katie's mother?	**Letter:** Have students write a letter from Katie to her mother explaining what has happened since the mother's death.

Vocabulary

subtle indirect; delicate; in a manner difficult to perceive or understand

Discussing the Short Story

1. List details from the story that show that Katie and her mother are strong. (Recall) *Her mom planned a birthday party for Katie when she was dying. Katie speaks fondly of all her mother has taught her.* (RL.6–12.3)

2. Why do you think it takes Katie a year to understand why her mother gave her the box? (Analysis) *Answers will vary. She has to go through a process of grieving. She is upset that her mother has seemingly given her nothing. She is feeling sorry for herself.*

3. List concrete actions Katie takes once she understands her mother's gift. (Analysis) *Students should list one or more of the following actions: She stops crying. She starts writing stories, poems, and memories. She finds herself.* (RL.6–12.3)

Special Focus: Symbolism

A *symbol* is a literary device in which an object stands for a more abstract idea or concept. For example, a rose can stand for love. Usually, literary symbols can be interpreted more than one way. In this story, the empty box is clearly symbolic. Katie, however, goes through several interpretations of it. Use the following questions to discuss the process of interpretation that Katie goes through. (SL.6–12.1)

- What does Katie think the box means when she first opens it? Why does she feel this way?
- What is her second interpretation?
- Do you think she will ever find another interpretation of the empty box? If so, what might it be?

Have students come up with other objects that can symbolize identity. You might prompt them with the following objects.

- a tree (we are always growing)
- an ocean (we can find out new things about ourselves by diving into the depths)
- a journey (we can discover who we are through experiencing new places or directions)

Cluster Four Vocabulary Test pages 112–142

Choose the meaning of the bold word in each passage.

1. She still had a lot of unresolved anger toward her first husband and it **manifested** itself in two ways . . . (*"Fairy Tale," p. 113*)

   (A) showed   (C) contradicted
   (B) hid   (D) resembled

2. "He pulls so hard on the leash that I could dislocate my shoulder. I'm **prone** to that, you know." (*"Fairy Tale," p. 114*)

   (A) afraid   (C) susceptible
   (B) immune   (D) victim

3. People were nicer there, softer and more **cognizant** of each other's feelings. (*"Fairy Tale," p. 115*)

   (A) caring   (C) callous
   (B) conniving   (D) aware

4. Even Sheri was in a clique of overweight girls who went around saying cleverly **snide** things about people and pretending they were Dorothy Parker. (*"Fairy Tale," p. 115*)

   (A) complimentary (C) sociable
   (B) nasty   (D) untrue

5. "You're the victim of divorce and remarriage, cast into these **opulent** premises by absentee parents who can't remember why they had children in the first place." (*"Fairy Tale," p. 116*)

   (A) wealthy   (C) secure
   (B) restrictive   (D) shabby

6. "Never forget that you're descended from **illustrious** ancestors, Andy." (*"Fox Hunt," p. 129*)

   (A) renowned   (C) corrupt
   (B) diligent   (D) mysterious

7. It was more interesting than coming from a long line of **decadent** aristocrats. (*"Fox Hunt," p. 130*)

   (A) mean   (C) self-indulgent
   (B) self-confident (D) angry

8. "It was made up by **malicious** neighbors who were jealous of the Liangs!" (*"Fox Hunt," p. 131*)

   (A) interfering   (C) elderly
   (B) well-meaning   (D) vicious

9. I don't want my mother to feel any loss of **prestige.** (*"Holly, age fifteen," p.136*)

   (A) trust   (C) confidence
   (B) dignity   (D) desire

10. She had guessed what might happen to me, had told me in a **subtle** way. (*"Birthday Box," p. 142*)

    (A) confusing   (C) indirect
    (B) obvious   (D) negative

Research, Writing, and Discussion Topics

The following are suggested topics you might research, write about, or discuss.

1. *Evaluate* this statement: "Everything that irritates us about others can lead us to an understanding of ourselves." State your opinion about whether you agree or disagree.

2. *Analyze* the characters in the book and decide which two have the strongest sense of identity. List three ways you could tell this for each character.

3. Use *generalization* to come up with a list of four common obstacles teenagers might encounter on the way to discovering their own identities.

4. *Analyze* how Tiffany, a person who has a strong personality, treats others. Tell why you would or would not feel comfortable being her friend.

5. *Evaluate* the role a parent plays in establishing a child's identity. Examine the parent-child relationships in "The Birthday Box" and "The Changeling."

6. *Analyze* the families in this book. All things considered, which family would you rather be a part of, and why?

7. Pick your favorite character from the stories in this book and *compare and contrast* your sense of identity with his or hers. What are the differences and similarities?

8. *Evaluate* the role peers play in establishing a person's identity. You might consider Jamie in "The Way Up" and Alan in "The Green Killer." In what ways are peers important to them?

9. *Synthesize* what you've learned about identity in this book. Write one statement—a single sentence—about what identity means to you.

10. Of the characters in this book, which two would you be most likely to see going out to dinner or attending a play by themselves? *Evaluate* what this says about them.

11. "Makeovers" with before and after pictures are popular features in magazines. *Analyze* what aspects of a person could be made over besides looks. List two of these aspects.

12. *Compare and contrast* the way boys feel about their image with the way girls feel about theirs. Work in small groups, using a collaborative writing environment such as Google Docs. Post your ideas so other members of your group can see them. Then coordinate with your group to pull the various ideas together into an essay. What differences and similarities exist?

13. *Evaluate* the ways in which a true friend respects another friend's identity.

14. Find a story or poem about identity. Write a review that *evaluates* whether the piece would make a good addition to this anthology.

Assessment and Project Ideas

Extended Research Opportunities

Here are some topics that you may wish to investigate further and report on either in writing or in an oral presentation to the class.

- celebrity identities: their right to privacy vs. the people's right to know
- the issue of cloning
- nature vs. nurture
- how people's self-images affect their health

Speaking and Listening

1. Create a dialogue between Moon from "Moon" and David Raymond from "On Being Seventeen, Bright, and Unable to Read." Have them discuss what makes them angry and how they handle their anger.
2. Write a response poem to "Getting Ready" that focuses on a teenage girl not caring what she wears or how she looks. Read the poem to the class.
3. Produce a mock talk show. Select a host and four classmates to pretend they are different characters from the book. The rest of the class can be the audience, asking the characters questions about identity, self-image, and why they made certain choices in their lives.
4. Using the poem "Side 32" as a model, write a song about what you are and what you are not.

Creative Writing

1. Write an additional scene to "The Way Up" in which Jamie's classmates discuss the tower-climbing stunt.
2. Write a poem describing your own sense of identity.
3. Write or find several *aphorisms,* or sayings, about self, identity, image, and personality. Organize your favorites into a collection.
4. Imagine that you are one of the characters in this anthology. Write a series of diary entries about your search for identity.
5. Write a dialogue on a crucial identity issue between one of the characters in this book and his or her parent.
6. Imagine that Jamie in "The Way Up" was injured while climbing the tower and write a newspaper editorial about the accident.

Multimedia Activities

1. Create an appropriate illustration for your favorite selection in this anthology.
2. Using materials such as photos, memorabilia, quotations, and poems, create a digital collage that tells who you are.
3. Write and perform a song about the importance of being yourself.
4. Draw a picture that could be used as the cover art for this book.
5. Take many photos of a friend or family member in various moods and expressions; then choose and display those that you think best capture aspects of your subject's identity.
6. As a team with other classmates, create a gallery of portraits of the main characters in this anthology. Use a collaborative tool such as Google Docs to upload your work and comment on one another's work.
7. Create and perform a dance expressing your own search for identity.

Answering the Essential Question

To help students prepare for the essay test on the following page, you may wish to reinforce the critical thinking skills presented in this book as students work through the mental tasks they must complete to answer the essential question. They can discuss the following questions either in small groups or as a whole class.

Defining

- What considerations are involved when you try to define your identity?
- To what extent can people change their identities?

Analyzing

- How many different kinds of identities, such as religious or racial, make up a whole person?
- In what ways do people rank the various categories of their identities?

Evaluating

- On what bases do you evaluate people?
- Are some categories of identity more important than others in evaluating a person's character?

Synthesizing

- How can you apply the understanding you have achieved from answering the previous questions to the essential question of this book: Who's the real you?

You may also wish to share the rubric for informative/expository writing found in the interactive whiteboard lesson, WhoAmI_4.4_CCSSRubric.

Essay Test

Using what you have learned while reading *Who Am I?* and what you already know, respond to the following question. This is an open-book test. Use quotations to support your response.

Prompt: Who's the real you?

Rubric for Project Evaluation: Grades 6–8

Apply those standards that fit the specific project. Some standards might not be used.

Standards	Criteria		
Areas of Assessment	Exceeds Standards	Meets Standards	Below Standards
Research Process • Focus • Search • Sources	❏ narrowed or broadened inquiry as needed ❏ used advanced search techniques ❏ assessed usefulness of each source ❏ synthesized multiple authoritative print and digital sources	❏ used focused questions for research ❏ used appropriate search techniques ❏ used multiple print and digital sources for longer projects ❏ evaluated credibility and accuracy of each source	❏ researched without clear focus ❏ relied on one or two sources only ❏ did not evaluate or recognize credibility and accuracy of sources
Writing Process • Planning through revising • Editing	❏ planned, drafted, revised, or rewrote to address key issues for purpose and audience ❏ edited to eliminate all errors in language conventions	❏ planned, drafted, revised, or rewrote to suit purpose and audience ❏ edited to eliminate all errors in language conventions	❏ did not refine work based on purpose and audience ❏ attempted editing but did not correct all errors in language conventions
Content • Ideas • Clarity • Suitability to task, purpose, and audience • Coherence • Style • Sources • Multimedia	❏ had a clear, interesting, well-developed main idea ❏ used effective organization for task, purpose, and audience ❏ used transitions well ❏ used a style appropriate for task, purpose, and audience ❏ selectively integrated evidence from sources for a smooth flow and cited accurately ❏ used digital media strategically to enhance findings, reasoning, and evidence, and to add interest	❏ had a clear, well-developed main idea ❏ used effective organization for task, purpose, and audience ❏ used transitions ❏ used style appropriate for task, purpose, and audience ❏ wove sources in smoothly and credited them ❏ used multimedia elements to clarify, add interest, and strengthen arguments	❏ main idea was unclear and support was weak ❏ organization was hard to follow ❏ used too few transitions ❏ used an inappropriate style ❏ did not cite sources or paraphrase correctly ❏ used few if any multimedia elements and they did not help strengthen the text
Oral Presentation • Ideas • Clarity • Points of view • Suitability to task, purpose, and audience • Speaking voice • Eye contact • Multimedia	❏ presented interesting ideas and information clearly so listeners could easily follow ❏ presented relevant and well-chosen evidence ❏ used organization, development, substance, and style appropriate for the task, purpose, and audience ❏ spoke expressively with adequate volume ❏ maintained good eye contact ❏ integrated digital media strategically	❏ emphasized the most important points ❏ was focused and coherent ❏ presented relevant and well-chosen evidence ❏ spoke with adequate volume ❏ maintained eye contact ❏ integrated multimedia	❏ did not clearly convey the most important points ❏ rambled somewhat ❏ did not present strong evidence ❏ was hard to hear ❏ did not keep good eye contact ❏ used few if any multimedia elements

Rubric for Project Evaluation: Grades 9–10

Apply those standards that fit the specific project. Some standards might not be used.

Standards	Criteria		
Areas of Assessment	Exceeds Standards	Meets Standards	Below Standards
Research Process • Focus • Search • Sources	❑ narrowed or broadened inquiry as needed ❑ used advanced search techniques ❑ assessed strengths and weaknesses of each source based on task, purpose, and audience ❑ synthesized multiple authoritative print and digital sources	❑ narrowed or broadened inquiry as needed ❑ used advanced search techniques ❑ assessed usefulness of each source ❑ synthesized multiple authoritative print and digital sources	❑ researched without clear focus ❑ used only obvious search techniques ❑ relied on just a few sources ❑ did not evaluate or recognize the usefulness of sources
Writing Process • Planning through revising • Editing	❑ planned, drafted, revised, or rewrote to address key issues for purpose and audience ❑ edited to eliminate all errors in language conventions	❑ planned, drafted, revised, or rewrote to address key issues for purpose and audience ❑ edited to eliminate all errors in language conventions	❑ did not refine work based on purpose and audience ❑ attempted editing but did not correct all errors in language conventions
Content • Ideas • Clarity • Suitability to task, purpose, and audience • Coherence • Style • Sources • Multimedia	❑ had a clear, meaningful main idea developed with outstanding and rich details and evidence ❑ used effective organization for task and purpose; audience appeal was high ❑ used transitions well ❑ used an engaging style appropriate for task, purpose, and audience ❑ selectively integrated solid evidence from multiple outstanding sources and cited accurately ❑ used creative digital media strategically to enhance findings, reasoning, and evidence, and to add interest	❑ had a clear, interesting, well-developed main idea ❑ used effective organization for task, purpose, and audience ❑ used transitions ❑ used a style appropriate for task, purpose, and audience ❑ selectively integrated evidence from sources for a smooth flow and cited accurately ❑ used digital media strategically to enhance findings, reasoning, and evidence, and to add interest	❑ main idea was somewhat unclear and was not well developed ❑ organization was hard to follow in places ❑ used too few transitions ❑ style could have been more appropriate for task, purpose, and audience ❑ included quotes from sources but did not integrate them smoothly and/or cite them accurately ❑ used too few and/or irrelevant multimedia elements
Oral Presentation • Ideas • Clarity • Points of view • Suitability to task, purpose, and audience • Speaking voice • Eye contact • Multimedia	❑ presented meaningful ideas and information clearly so listeners could easily follow ❑ conveyed a clear and distinct perspective ❑ addressed alternate perspectives ❑ used organization, development, substance, and style appropriate for the task, purpose, and audience ❑ spoke expressively with adequate volume ❑ maintained excellent eye contact ❑ integrated digital media strategically	❑ presented interesting ideas and information clearly so listeners could easily follow ❑ presented relevant and well-chosen evidence ❑ used organization, development, substance, and style appropriate for the task, purpose, and audience ❑ spoke expressively with adequate volume ❑ maintained good eye contact ❑ integrated digital media strategically	❑ did not clearly convey the most important points ❑ rambled in places ❑ not all evidence was strong ❑ was hard to hear at times ❑ did not keep good eye contact ❑ did not tie multimedia elements closely enough to presentation

Rubric for Project Evaluation: Grades 11–12

Apply those standards that fit the specific project. Some standards might not be used.

Standards	Criteria		
Areas of Assessment	Exceeds Standards	Meets Standards	Below Standards
Research Process • Focus • Search • Sources	❏ adapted research to changing understandings based on progressive learning from sources ❏ used advanced search techniques, tapping into authoritative databases ❏ used five or more sources, including primary sources and interviews when useful	❏ narrowed or broadened inquiry as needed ❏ used advanced search techniques ❏ assessed strengths and weaknesses of each source based on task, purpose, and audience ❏ synthesized multiple authoritative print and digital sources	❏ researched without clear focus ❏ used only obvious search techniques ❏ relied on just a few sources ❏ did not evaluate or recognize the usefulness of sources
Writing Process • Planning through revising • Editing	❏ planned, drafted, revised, or rewrote to address key issues for purpose and audience ❏ edited to eliminate all errors in language conventions ❏ edited creatively to enhance style and readability	❏ planned, drafted, revised, or rewrote to address key issues for purpose and audience ❏ edited to eliminate all errors in language conventions	❏ did not refine work based on purpose and audience ❏ attempted editing but did not correct all errors in language conventions
Content • Ideas • Clarity • Suitability to task, purpose, and audience • Coherence • Style • Sources • Multimedia	❏ had a clear, meaningful main idea developed with complex and complete evidence ❏ crafted creative, effective organization; audience appeal was high ❏ used sophisticated transitions ❏ used a compelling style appropriate for task, purpose, and audience ❏ selectively integrated solid evidence from multiple outstanding sources and cited accurately ❏ used creative digital media strategically ❏ conveyed depth of personal interest in subject	❏ had a clear, meaningful main idea developed with outstanding and rich details and evidence ❏ used effective organization for task and purpose; audience appeal was high ❏ used transitions well ❏ used an engaging style appropriate for task, purpose, and audience ❏ selectively integrated solid evidence from multiple outstanding sources and cited accurately ❏ used creative digital media strategically to enhance findings, reasoning, and evidence, and to add interest	❏ main idea was somewhat unclear and was not well developed in places ❏ organization was logical but lacked transitions ❏ used too few transitions ❏ style could have been more appropriate for task, purpose, and audience ❏ included quotes from sources but did not integrate them smoothly and/or cite them accurately ❏ used multimedia elements that did not always enhance or strengthen presentation
Oral Presentation • Ideas • Clarity • Points of view • Suitability to task, purpose, and audience • Speaking voice • Eye contact • Multimedia	❏ presented meaningful ideas and information clearly and creatively ❏ conveyed a clear, distinct, and involved perspective ❏ addressed alternate perspectives ❏ used organization, development, substance, and style very well suited for the task, purpose, and audience ❏ spoke expressively with adequate volume and used gestures and movement to reinforce key points ❏ maintained excellent eye contact and adjusted to audience reactions ❏ integrated digital media strategically	❏ presented meaningful ideas and information clearly so listeners could easily follow ❏ conveyed a clear and distinct perspective ❏ addressed alternate perspectives ❏ used organization, development, substance, and style appropriate for the task, purpose, and audience ❏ spoke expressively with adequate volume ❏ maintained excellent eye contact ❏ integrated digital media strategically	❏ did not clearly convey the most important points ❏ rambled in places ❏ not all evidence was strong ❏ was hard to hear at times ❏ did not keep good eye contact ❏ did not tie multimedia elements closely enough to presentation

Related Literature

Choose from the following selections to enhance and extend the themes in this *Literature &
Thought* anthology. The letters *RL* in the brackets indicate the reading level of the book listed.
IL indicates the approximate interest level. Perfection Learning's catalog numbers are included for
your ordering convenience.

Challenging

The Catcher in the Rye by J.D. Salinger. A perceptive study of adolescent Holden Caulfield.
Exceptional realism appeals to high school students. [RL 9 IL 10–12] Paperback 0198001;
Cover Craft 0198002.

A Separate Peace by John Knowles. Story of a lonely introvert and his rival, a daredevil athlete,
and what happens at school. [RL 8 IL 7 +] Paperback 0743001; Cover Craft 0743002.

Average

The Chocolate War by Robert Cormier. A high school boy refuses to be intimidated by the
society and people around him. [RL 8 IL 9–12] Paperback 9095301; Cover Craft 9095302.

Dogsong by Gary Paulsen. Inspired by an Eskimo shaman, Russel takes a dog team and sled to
escape the modern ways of his village and to find the "song" of himself. [RL 7 IL 5–9]
Paperback 8900001; Cover Craft 8900002.

Hoop Dreams: A True Story by Ben Joravsky. The urban struggle to NBA glory of Arthur Agee
and William Gates. Includes updated information about the Best Documentary Award-winning
film based on this book. [RL 7 IL 8 +] Paperback 4939901; Cover Craft 4939902.

The Midwife's Apprentice by Karen Cushman. In medieval England, a homeless girl finds her
place in the world. [RL 6 IL 7 +] Paperback 4918001; Cover Craft 4918002.

Runs with Horses by Brian Burks. Runs with Horses is a member of the last, small group of
Apaches continuing to resist capture by the U.S. Army. His training for manhood does not
prepare him for the threat of surrender. [RL 6 IL 7–9] Paperback 4938501; Cover Craft
4938502.

Scorpions by Walter Dean Myers. Friendship with young Tito provides ballast for 12-year-old
Jamal as his family struggles in Harlem; as he becomes alienated at school; and as members of
his incarcerated brother's street gang, the Scorpions, move in on him. [RL 6 IL 7–12]
Paperback 4062101; Cover Craft 4062102.

What Hearts by Bruce Brooks. Four interrelated stories about significant moments in the life of
a brilliant boy named Asa who learns about baseball, survival, and the power of the words of
love. [RL 6 IL 5–9] Paperback 4587201; Cover Craft 4587202.

Z for Zachariah by Robert C. O'Brien. A novel about the aftermath of nuclear devastation.
[RL 6.5 IL 7–12] Paperback 8999301; Cover Craft 8999302.

Easy

Belle Prater's Boy by Ruth White. Everyone in Coal Station, Virginia, has a theory about what
happened to Belle Prater, but 12-year-old Gypsy wants the facts. [RL 4.7 IL 4–9] Paperback
5520501; Cover Craft 5520502.

The Star Fisher by Laurence Yep. When a Chinese American family moves to West Virginia to
open a laundry and start new lives, they find that not everyone in town is ready to welcome
them. With courage and a sense of humor, they show that they are there to stay. [RL 5 IL 5–9]
Paperback 4381501; Cover Craft 4381502.

What Do You Know?

You are about to begin a unit on the theme of identity. Mark the following true/false statements by putting a "T" or "F" on the lines. This is not a test. Think of it as a way to find out what you feel about the themes and issues related to identity.

True or False

_____ 1. Your personality stays basically the same throughout your life.

_____ 2. The way people treat you affects who you think you are.

_____ 3. It's really important to fit in with other people.

_____ 4. You should say what you really think, no matter what.

_____ 5. It feels good to be popular.

_____ 6. If you are yourself, people will like you.

_____ 7. It's easier to get friends when you are going steady.

_____ 8. Being adopted makes it more difficult to find out who you are.

_____ 9. It's natural for people to be mean to unattractive people.

_____10. Smart people aren't popular.

ANSWERS

Cluster One Vocabulary Test (page 26)

1. B; **2.** C; **3.** B; **4.** D; **5.** D; **6.** C; **7.** D; **8.** D; **9.** B; **10.** A

Cluster Two Vocabulary Test (page 37)

1. A; **2.** C; **3.** B; **4.** D; **5.** A; **6.** B; **7.** B; **8.** C; **9.** C; **10.** C

Cluster Three Vocabulary Test (page 47)

1. A; **2.** A; **3.** B; **4.** C; **5.** A; **6.** C; **7.** D; **8.** C; **9.** B; **10.** A

Cluster Four Vocabulary Test (page 57)

1. A; **2.** B; **3.** D; **4.** C; **5.** A; **6.** A; **7.** B; **8.** D; **9.** C; **10.** B